Fodo
Alaska
Ports of Call

Portions of this book appear in F

Fodor's Travel Publications
New York • Toronto • London • Sydney • Auckland
www.fodors.com

Fodor's Alaska Ports of Call

Editor: Mary Beth Bohman

Editorial Contributors: Sue Kernaghan, Melissa Klurman, Don Pitcher, Sarah Sper

Maps: David Lindroth, *cartographer;* Bob Blake and Rebecca Baer, *map editors*

Design: Fabrizio La Rocca, *creative director;* Tigest Getachew, *art director;* Melanie Marin, *senior picture editor*

Production/Manufacturing: Robert B. Shields

Cover Photo: Holland America Line (top photo), Johnny Johnson/AlaskaStock.com (bottom photo)

Cover Design: Allison Saltzman

Copyright

Sixth Edition

ISBN 1–4000–1306–2

ISSN 1520–0205

Special Sales

CONTENTS

4   Shore Excursions   *151*

Index   *161*

Maps

Don't Forget to Write

Your experiences—positive and negative—matter to us. If we have missed or misstated something, we want to hear about it. We follow up on all suggestions. Contact the *Alaska Ports of Call* editor at editors@fodors.com or c/o Fodor's, 1745 Broadway, New York, NY 10019. And have a fabulous trip!

Important Tip

Although all prices, opening times, and other details in this book are based on information supplied to us at press time, changes occur all the time in the travel world, and Fodor's cannot accept responsibility for facts that become outdated or for inadvertent errors or omissions. So **always confirm information when it matters,** especially if you're making a detour to visit a specific place.

Karen Cure
Editorial Director

THE CHARACTER OF ALASKA

If you're considering a cruise to Alaska, chances are you're already enchanted by the imagery associated with the 49th American state. After all, "The Great Land," a loose translation of the Aleut word *Alyeska,* boasts the highest mountain in North America—Denali—as well as 17 of the 20 highest peaks in the United States. There are more bald eagles here than anywhere else, more totem poles, thousands of glaciers, king-size salmon, and humongous halibut.

Geography alone makes Alaska an ideal cruise destination. Except for those in and around Haines and Skagway in the north, there are no roads linking the towns along the Panhandle. In fact, Juneau is the only state capital in the United States that cannot be reached over land. You fly in or you sail in, but you don't drive in. And the nature of ship travel is perfectly suited to discovering what Alaska is all about. From the deck of a cruise ship, you can come face to face with a glacier. From the dining room, you can watch a full moon rise over a snow-striped mountain. And you can enjoy it all in the lap of luxury.

The natural beauty of Alaska is hard to overstate. As you prepare for your cruise, consider these facts about Alaska's grandeur: the Inside Passage, the traditional route north to Alaska, stretches 1,000 mi from Puget Sound, Washington, in the south, to Skagway, Alaska, in the north. From there, the Gulf of Alaska arcs for another 500 mi from east to west. Alaska has thousands of glaciers. No one really knows how many, but estimates range from 5,000 to 100,000. Among the most famous ones that cruise passengers visit are LeConte outside Petersburg, the southernmost calving glacier in North America, and Hubbard at Yakutat Bay in the Gulf of Alaska, 6 mi wide and 76 mi long to its source. Tongass National Forest, which spans great stretches of the Inside Passage, is the largest national forest in the United States. Wrangell-St. Elias National Park, a UNESCO World Heritage Site east of Anchorage and bordering the Gulf of Alaska, is the largest national park in the United States—six times the size of Yellowstone.

Wildlife is everywhere in Alaska. Southeast Alaska has more brown bears than the rest of the United States combined. And Alaska ranks number one in bald eagles. Bird-watchers will have a field day looking for them perched high in the treetops—or atop telephone poles—all along the Inside Passage. In fact, eagles are so numerous here you'll have to remind yourself that they remain a threatened species.

You may also come across whales during your cruise. If so, your captain may cut the ship's engines so as not to disturb them and to allow you some time to observe them. The state has 15 species of whales. And don't be surprised if you see a bear foraging on the shoreline. Such are the simple pleasures of an Alaskan cruise: calving glaciers, sea lions and seals, and sensational sunsets—at midnight.

In addition to glaciers and wildlife, there's an exciting frontier history to discover. Scientists estimate that the first people arrived in Alaska some 15,000 years ago, when they migrated across the Bering Land Bridge from Asia. The earliest evidence of human habitation along the Inside Passage can be found in Wrangell, where petroglyphs—mysterious markings carved into rocks and boulders on the beach—are thought to be at least 8,000 years old.

Alaska's indigenous people belong to one of four groups: Aleuts, Athabascans, Eskimos, and Northwest Coast Indians. The Aleuts live on the Aleutian Islands. Athabascans populate the Interior, while Eskimos inhabit the Arctic regions of the Far North. The Native Alaskans you are most likely to meet during your cruise are the Tlingit, Haida, or Tsimshian people of the Inside Passage.

The Tlingit are responsible for Alaska's famous totem carvings. Totem poles tell the story of a great event, identify members of the same clan, and honor great leaders. Today you can still see native artisans at work on totem poles in Ketchikan, Haines, and Sitka. Miniature totem reproductions are among the most popular souvenirs in Alaska, but ceremonial masks, decorative paddles, and woven baskets also make great gifts.

Buying local crafts is just one way for cruise passengers to appreciate the local culture. Native Alaskans are often happy to show you around. In Juneau, Ketchikan, and Sitka, you can book a sightseeing tour with a native point of view. Performances of native dance and traditional storytelling entertain visitors in Juneau, Sitka, and Haines.

In the footsteps of Native Alaskans came European explorers. The first was Vitus Bering, who "discovered" Alaska and claimed it for Russia in 1741. Next came British and Spanish explorers. Cook Inlet in Anchorage is named for British explorer Captain Cook. One member of Cook's expedition was George Vancouver, namesake of the Canadian port city where most Alaska cruises begin or end. Wrangell Island, at the southern end of the Inside Passage, is the only Alaskan port of call to have flown three flags—Russian, British, and finally American.

The connection with Europe is echoed in the nicknames given to some of Alaska's port cities. Valdez is often referred to as Alaska's Little Switzerland for the mountains that ring the city. Petersburg is Alaska's Little Norway. The town's residents still celebrate their Scandinavian heritage every May in a festival of Norwegian song and dance.

Russia sold Alaska to the United States in 1867 for $7.2 million, or about 2¢ an acre. Secretary of State William H. Seward, who orchestrated the purchase, was publicly ridiculed for his "folly." But opinions changed when word got out that gold had been discovered in the Far North; the news set off a stampede of legendary proportion. The gold rush, perhaps the most colorful episode in Alaska's storied history, put Alaska on the map, as gold-crazed prospectors, con men, and assorted other characters headed up the Inside Passage.

If you're an aficionado of gold-rush history, choose a cruise that includes a call at Skagway, the gateway to the Klondike of a century ago. As you sail the Lynn Canal, the natural channel that connects Skagway with the rest of the Inside Passage, keep in mind that you are following the same route and traveling in the same manner (albeit a bit more luxuriously) as the original prospectors. Today Skagway looks much as it did in the early 1900s. The entire downtown area is a National Historic District. Be sure to take a ride on the vintage parlor cars of the White Pass and Yukon Railway. It's one of the few chances cruise passengers have to venture deep into the mountains—just as prospectors traveled over the treacherous White Pass.

As you are about to discover, cruising is a great way to see "The Great Land." Spend as much time as you can in Alaska. Bring plenty of film or videotape, don't forget a rain slicker, and do try everything. Go hiking and fishing. Ride the railroads, book a salmon bake, scope for eagles. Think big—and be sure to buy a souvenir totem pole.

1 Cruise Primer

IF YOU HAVEN'T CRUISED BEFORE, you may be anxious about choosing and booking a cruise. With all of the lines, ships, and itineraries out there, the choices can seem mind-boggling. If you feel overwhelmed, what you need is a strategy. With a game plan, choosing a line, a ship, and an itinerary becomes easy. Divide the work up into steps and forge ahead.

You have to know what you want in order to find it. You also have to be able to explain yourself to a travel agent or make your own decisions when booking a cruise yourself on-line. So take an inventory of your priorities: What sort of rhythm do you want—rest and relaxation at sea or excursions in new ports every day? Do you want a big, extravagant ship or a smaller, simpler one? Do you want all-out luxury or a barefoot and budget trip? Do you want to get dressed up for dinner every night, or do you want to dine as you are? Do you want to go to bed early or dance the night away? What do you want out of your days? Enrichment or entertainment? Roulette or relaxation? Maybe a little of both? No single ship has everything, but you can narrow down the field to a few that fit the bill.

The more you know, the easier it will be to make your choice. So get as much information as possible. Begin by getting recommendations from friends and coworkers who have taken cruises. What did or didn't they like about their ship? Would they take the same cruise again? Friends and family provide the best recommendations, because they're most likely to know what you would like.

Next, visit or call more than one cruise-only travel agency and ask for suggestions. CLIA (Cruise Line International Association) travel agents have information about all types of ships and are likely to know about ships that your friends and family may not be aware of. Ask each agent to send you brochures for the recommended ships. Be aware that many travel agents work exclusively with certain cruise lines. One agency may specialize in Carnival, NCL, and Holland America, another in Princess. But the agency that sells more Holland America cruises will usually be able to offer you better prices on those cruises.

When leafing through brochures, take a good look at the photographs—not just the cabins and deck layout but the pictures of people. A cruise geared toward senior citizens won't be promoted with shots of twentysomethings in its brochure. For instance, Carnival shows lots of younger couples and families with children, while Royal Caribbean shows a mix of ages, often in the same shot. Celebrity shows chic people in stylish settings. Brochures and their video and electronic equivalents, along with Web sites, are the most useful tools for planning a cruise. All give you valuable information about what you will and won't find on board.

BEFORE YOU GO

Once you have chosen your cruise and signed on to go, it's time to get ready. Preparations for a cruise may involve many distinct tasks, but none of them are difficult, especially if broken down into manageable steps. Most important, allow plenty of time to get ready so you don't get harried in the last couple of weeks.

Tickets and Vouchers

After you make the final payment to your travel agent, the cruise line will issue your cruise tickets and vouchers for airport–ship transfers. Depending on the airline, and whether you have purchased an air-sea package, you may receive your plane tickets or charter-flight vouchers at the same time; you may also receive vouchers for any shore excursions, although most cruise lines issue these aboard ship. Should your travel documents not arrive when promised, contact your travel agent or cruise line. If you book late, tickets may be delivered directly to the ship.

Passports and Visas

For Alaska cruises, whether they begin in the U.S. or in Canada, American and Canadian citizens require proof of citizenship. A valid passport, though not required, is the best document to carry. If you do not have a passport, take a certified copy of your birth certificate, which must have a raised seal, and some form of photo identification. Permanent residents of the U.S. who are not citizens should carry their green card.

If you are a citizen of another country, you may be required to obtain visas in advance. It is always the responsibility of the person traveling to obtain the necessary travel documents, including visas. Check with your travel agent or cruise line about specific requirements. If you do need a visa for your cruise, your travel agent should be able to help you obtain it, but there may be a charge for this service, in addition to the visa charge. Read your cruise documents carefully to see what documents you'll need for embarkation. You don't want to be turned away at the pier.

Immigration regulations require every passenger boarding a cruise ship from a U.S. port to provide additional personal data, such as your current mailing address and telephone number, to the cruise operator in advance of embarkation. Failure to provide this information required by the U.S. government may result in denial of boarding.

Disabilities and Accessibility

The latest cruise ships have been built with the needs of travelers with disabilities in mind, and many older ships have been modified to accommodate them. But several cruise lines operate older ships that have not been modified or do not have elevators: the tall sailing ships and explorer-type vessels are not the easiest ships to navigate if you are in a wheelchair. The key areas to be concerned about are public rooms, outer decks, and, of course, your cabin.

If you need a specially equipped cabin, book as far in advance as possible and ask questions of your travel agent or a cruise-line representative. Specifically, ask how your cabin is configured and equipped. Is the entrance level or ramped? Are all doorways at least 30″ wide (wider if your wheelchair is not standard)? Are pathways to beds, closets, and bathrooms at least 36″ wide and unobstructed? In the bathroom, is there 42″ of clear space in front of the toilet and are there grab bars behind and on one side of it and in the bathtub and shower? Are elevators wide enough to accommodate wheelchairs?

The best cruise ship for passengers who use wheelchairs is one that ties up right at the dock at every port, at which time a ramp or even an elevator is always made available. Unfortunately, it's hard to ascertain this in advance, since a ship may tie up at the dock at one port on one voyage and, on the next, anchor in the harbor and have passengers transported to shore via tender. Ask your travel agent to find out which ships are capable of docking. If a tender is used, some ships will have crew members carry the wheelchair and passenger from the ship to the tender. Unfortunately, other ships will refuse to take wheelchairs on tenders, especially if the water is choppy.

What to Pack

Certain packing rules apply to all cruises. Always take along a sweater to counter cool evening ocean breezes or overactive air-conditioning. A rain slicker is essential—many travelers who plan on indulging in some of the more active shore excursions pack a complete rain suit. Be prepared to dress in layers, since temperatures can vary considerably during the day. Make sure you take at least one pair of comfortable walking shoes for exploring port towns, and waterproof footwear will be useful as well. Ankle-high rubber boots are ideal for many shore trips.

Generally speaking, plan on one outfit for every two days of cruising, especially if your wardrobe contains many interchangeable pieces. Ships often have laundry facilities. Don't forget your toiletries and sundry items, but if you do, these are readily available in port shops or the ship's gift shop (though usually at a premium price). Cabin amenities typically include soap and often shampoo, conditioner, and other lotions and potions.

Outlets in cabin bathrooms are usually compatible with U.S.-purchased appliances. This may not be the case on older ships or those with European registries; call ahead if this is a concern for you. Most cabin bathrooms are equipped with low-voltage outlets for electric shavers, and many newer ships have built-in hair dryers.

Take an extra pair of eyeglasses or contact lenses in your carry-on luggage. If you use a prescription drug, pack enough to last the duration of the trip or have your doctor write a prescription using the drug's generic name, because brand names vary from country to country. Always carry medications in their original packaging to avoid problems with customs officials. Don't pack them in luggage that you plan to check, in case your bags go astray. Pack a list of the offices that supply refunds for lost or stolen traveler's checks. Make a copy of your passport and keep it separate from your actual passport. If you should lose your passport or it is stolen, having a copy of it can greatly facilitate replacement. Make copies, or write down the numbers, of your credit cards in case those should be lost or stolen.

FORMAL/SEMIFORMAL/CASUAL

Although no two cruises are quite the same, evening dress tends to fall into three categories.

Formal cruises celebrate the ceremony of cruising. Jackets and ties for men are the rule for dinner, tuxedos are not uncommon, and the dress code is observed faithfully throughout the evening.

Semiformal cruises are a bit more relaxed than their formal counterparts. Men wear jackets and ties most nights.

Casual cruises are the most popular. Shipboard dress and lifestyle are informal. Men wear sport shirts and slacks to dinner most nights and don jackets and ties only two or three evenings of a typical seven-day sailing.

In today's casual-Friday world, most cruise lines have reduced the focus on formal and semiformal dining and offer multiple dining options, including room service. However, it would be wise to ask the cruise line about its dining dress code so you know what to expect and what to pack.

ARRIVING AND DEPARTING

If you have purchased an air-sea package, you will be met by a cruise-company representative when your plane lands at the port city and then shuttled directly to the ship in a bus or minivan. Some cruise lines arrange to transport luggage between airport and ship so passengers don't have to deal with baggage claim at the start of your cruise or with baggage check-in at the end. If you decide not to buy the air-sea package but still plan to fly, ask your travel agent if you can use the ship's transfer bus. Otherwise, you will have to take a taxi to the ship.

If you live close to the port of embarkation, bus transportation may be available. If you are part of a group that has booked a cruise together, this transportation may be part of your package. Another option for those who live close to their point of departure is to drive to the ship, an increasingly popular option. Major U.S. cruise ports all have parking facilities.

Embarkation

Check-In

On arrival at the dock, you must check in before boarding your ship. An officer will collect or stamp your ticket, inspect or even retain your passport or other official identification, ask you to fill out a tourist card, check that you have the correct visas, and collect any unpaid port or departure tax.

Seating assignments for the dining room are often handed out at this time, too, although most cruise ships are now offering you the opportunity to dine when and with whom you like in any of several restaurants aboard. You may also register your credit card to open a shipboard account, or that may be done later at the purser's office.

After this, you will be required to go through a security check and to pass your hand baggage through an x-ray inspection. These are the same machines in use at airports, so ask to have your photographic film inspected by hand.

Although it takes only 5 or 10 minutes per family to check in, lines are often long, so aim for off-peak hours. The worst time tends to be immediately after the ship begins boarding; the later it is, the less crowded. For example, if boarding is from 2 to 4:30, lines are shorter after 3:30.

Boarding the Ship

Before you walk up the gangway, the ship's photographer will probably take your picture; there's no charge unless you buy the picture (usually $7 to $8). Onboard, stewards may serve welcome drinks in souvenir glasses—for which you're usually charged between $3 and $5.

You will either be escorted to your cabin by a steward or, on a smaller ship, given your key—now usually a plastic card—by a ship's officer and directed to your cabin. Some elevators are unavailable to passengers during boarding, since they are used to transport luggage. You may arrive to find your luggage outside your cabin or just inside the door; if it hasn't arrived a half hour before sailing, contact the purser. If your luggage doesn't make it to the ship in time, the purser will have it flown to the next port.

Visitors' Passes

A few cruise ships permit passengers to invite guests on board prior to sailing, although nowadays most lines prohibit all but paying passengers from boarding for reasons of security and insurance liability. Cruise companies that allow visitors usually require that you obtain passes several weeks in advance; call the line for policies and procedures.

Most ships do not allow visitors while the ship is docked in a port of call. If you meet a friend on shore, you won't be able to invite him or her back to your stateroom.

Disembarkation

The last night of your cruise is full of business. On most ships you must place everything except your hand luggage outside your door, ready to be picked up by midnight or early in the morning. Color-coded tags, distributed to your cabin in a debarkation packet, should be placed on your luggage before the crew collects it. The color of your tag will determine when you leave the ship and help you retrieve your luggage on the pier.

Your shipboard bill is left in your room during the last day of a cruise or on the morning of your departure from the ship; to pay the bill (if you haven't already put it on your credit card) or to settle any questions, you must stand in line at the purser's office. Tips to the cabin steward and dining staff are distributed on the last night of the cruise or are automatically added to your onboard account. On many ships, you can review your account on your in-cabin television and change those tips in any way you like, up or down. You may also make changes to or discuss your bill at the purser's office at any time during the cruise. Some ships will deliver your account to your room the morning of your departure. If you have not already paid it by credit card or wish to dispute any charges on it, go to the purser immediately to settle or discuss your account. Do not wait until you're ready to get off the ship, as lines may be long and the wait could delay your departure and fray your nerves. Some lines close down their computer files for the cruise by 9 AM or 10 AM to prepare for the next cruise and may be unable to credit your account with any disputed charges, requiring you to contact your credit-card company or the cruise line later for a refund.

On the morning the cruise ends, in-room breakfast service may not be available because stewards are too busy, but you will usually find breakfast being served in both the formal dining room and at the ship's buffet dining area. Most passengers clear out of their cabins as soon as possible, gather their hand luggage, and stake out a chair in one of the public lounges to await the ship's clearance through customs. Be patient—it takes a long time to unload and sort thousands of pieces of luggage.

Passengers are disembarked in groups according to color-coded luggage tags; those with the earliest flights get off first. If you have a tight connection, notify the purser before the last day, and he or she may be able to arrange faster pre-clearing and debarkation.

Customs and Duties

U.S. Customs

Before a ship lands, each individual or family must fill out a customs declaration, regardless of whether they purchased anything abroad. If your purchases total less than $400, you will not need to itemize them. Be prepared to pay whatever duties are owed directly to the customs inspector, with cash or check. Be sure to keep receipts for all purchases, and be ready to show curious officials what you've bought.

U.S. Customs pre-clears some ships—it's done on the ship before you disembark. In other ports you must collect your luggage from the dock, then stand in line to pass through the inspection point. This can take up to an hour.

ALLOWANCES

U.S. residents who have been out of the country for at least 48 hours may bring home, for personal use, $800 worth of foreign goods duty-free, as long as they haven't used the $800 allowance or any part of it in the past 30 days. This exemption may include 1 liter of alcohol (for travelers 21 and older), 200 cigarettes, and 100 non-Cuban cigars. Family members from the same household who are traveling together may pool their $800 personal exemptions. For fewer than 48 hours, the duty-free allowance drops to $200, which may include 50 cigarettes, 10 non-Cuban cigars, and 150 ml of alcohol (or perfume containing alcohol). The $200 allowance cannot be combined with other individuals' exemptions, and if you exceed it, the full value of all the goods will be taxed. Antiques, which the U.S. Bureau of Customs and Border Protection defines as objects more than 100 years old, enter duty-free, as do original works of art done entirely by hand, including paintings, drawings, and sculptures. This doesn't apply to folk art or handicrafts, which are in general dutiable.

SENDING PACKAGES HOME

You may also send packages home duty-free, with a limit of one parcel per addressee per day (except alcohol or tobacco products or perfume worth more than $5). You can mail up to $200 worth of goods for personal use; label the package PERSONAL USE and attach a list of its contents and their retail value. If the package contains your used personal belongings, mark it PERSONAL GOODS RETURNED to avoid paying duties. You may send up to $100 worth of goods as a gift; mark the package UNSOLICITED GIFT. Mailed items do not affect your duty-free allowance on your return.

U.S. CUSTOMS FOR FOREIGNERS

If you hold a foreign passport and will be returning home within hours of docking, you may be exempt from all U.S. Customs duties. Everything you bring into the United States must leave with you when you return home. When you reach your own country, you will have to pay duties there.

Canadian Customs

Canadian residents who have been out of Canada for at least seven days may bring in C$750 worth of goods duty-free. If you've been away fewer than seven days but more than 48 hours, the duty-free allowance drops to C$200. If your trip lasts 24 to 48 hours, the allowance is C$50. You may not pool allowances with family members. Goods claimed under the C$750 exemption may follow you by mail; those claimed under the lesser exemptions must accompany you. Alcohol and tobacco products may be included in the seven-day and 48-hour exemptions but not in the 24-hour exemption. If you meet the age requirements of the province or territory through which you reenter Canada, you may bring in, duty-free, 1.5 liters of wine *or* 1.14 liters (40 imperial ounces) of liquor *or* 24 12-ounce cans or bottles of beer or ale. Also, if you meet the local age requirement for tobacco products, you may bring in, duty-free, 200 cigarettes and 50 cigars. Check ahead of time with the Canada Customs and Revenue Agency or the Department of Agriculture for policies regarding meat products, seeds, plants, and fruits.

You may send an unlimited number of gifts (only one gift per recipient, however) worth up to C$60 each duty-free to Canada. Label the package UNSOLICITED GIFT—VALUE UNDER $60. Alcohol and tobacco are excluded.

U.K. Customs

From countries outside the European Union, including the United States, you may bring home, duty-free, 200 cigarettes or 50 cigars; 1 liter of spirits or 2 liters of fortified or sparkling wine or liqueurs; 2 liters of still table wine; 60 ml of perfume; 250 ml of toilet water; plus £145 worth of other goods, including gifts and souvenirs. Prohibited items include meat products, seeds, plants, and fruits.

ON BOARD

Checking Out Your Cabin

The first thing to do upon arriving at your cabin or suite is to make sure that everything is in order. If there are two twin beds instead of the double bed you wanted—or other problems—ask to be moved before the ship departs. Unless the ship is full, you can usually persuade the chief housekeeper or hotel manager to allow you to change cabins. It is customary to tip the stewards who help you move. In most modern ships, beds can be pushed together to create one single bed or moved apart for two. Ask your cabin steward to set the beds up the way you would like them or to move you to another room.

Since your cabin is your home away from home for a few days or weeks, everything should be to your satisfaction. Take a good look around: is the cabin clean and orderly? Do the toilet, shower, and faucets work? Check the telephone and television. Again, major problems should be addressed immediately. Minor concerns, such as a shortage of pillows, can wait until the frenzy of embarkation subsides.

Your dining-time and seating-assignment card may be in your cabin; now is the time to check it and immediately request any changes. The maître d' usually sets up shop in one of the public rooms specifically for this purpose.

Shipboard Accounts

Virtually all cruise ships operate as cashless societies. Passengers charge onboard purchases and settle their accounts at the end of the cruise with a credit card, traveler's checks, or cash. You can sign for wine at dinner, drinks at the bar, shore excursions, gifts in the shop—virtually any expense you may incur aboard ship. On some lines, an imprint from a major credit card is necessary to open an account. Otherwise, a cash deposit may be required and a positive balance maintained to keep the shipboard account open. Either way, you will want to open a line of credit soon after settling in, if an account was not opened for you at embarkation. This can easily be arranged by visiting the purser's office, in the central atrium or main lobby. On most ships, you can now view your account at any time on your in-cabin television. To make your stay aboard as seamless—and as cashless—as possible, many cruise lines now add dining-room gratuities at a set rate to your onboard account. Some lines offer access to personal records via Internet; you can alter automatic tips, for example, before your cruise begins.

Tipping

For better or worse, tipping is an integral part of the cruise experience. Most companies pay their cruise staff nominal wages and expect tips to make up the difference between this nominal amount and a living wage. Most cruise lines have recommended tipping guidelines, and on many ships "voluntary" tipping for beverage service has been replaced with a mandatory 15% service charge, which is added to every bar bill. On the other hand, the most expensive luxury lines include tips in the cruise fare and may prohibit crew members from accepting additional gratuities. On many small adventure ships, a collection box is placed in the dining room or lounge on the last full day of the cruise, and passengers contribute anonymously.

Some large cruise lines now add dining-room tips of $10 to $12 a person per day directly to your bill. That sum is intended to cover all your dining-room service, other than the wine steward and the maître d' if he provides special service to you (although both those may also be included in the daily tip that is automatically added to your account); it may also include your room steward. Ask the purser if tips are being added to your bill and which personnel will receive them—waiter, busboy, and room steward are all expecting tips. You may adjust tips up or down.

Dining

Ocean liners serve food nearly around the clock. There may be as many as four breakfast options: early-morning coffee and pastries on deck, breakfast in bed through room service, buffet-style dining in the cafeteria, and a more formal breakfast in the dining room. There may also be several lunch choices, midafternoon hors d'oeuvres, teatime, and late-night buffets. You may eat whatever is on the menu, in any quantity, at any meal. Room service is traditionally, but not always, free (⇨ Shipboard Services, *below*).

Restaurants

The chief meals of the day are served in the main dining room, which on most ships can accommodate only half the passengers at once. Meals are therefore usually served in early (or main) and late (or second) seatings. Early seating for dinner is generally between 6 and 6:30, late seating between 8 and 8:30.

Most cruise ships have a buffet-style restaurant, usually near the swimming pool, where you can eat breakfast and lunch. On many of the newer ships, that room, nearly always on the Lido Deck near the swimming pool, becomes a casual, waiter-service dining room at dinner. Those dining rooms, often featuring grilled specialties, are popular on nights when the ship has been in port all day. Many ships provide self-serve coffee or tea in their cafeteria around the clock, as well as midnight buffets.

Some ships, particularly newer ones, also have alternative specialty restaurants for which a reservation must be made. You might have to pay a fee for grilled steak or Asian cuisine. On-demand food shops may include pizzerias, ice cream parlors, and caviar or cappuccino bars; there may be an extra charge at these facilities, too.

Smoking is often banned in main dining rooms. At least one cruise line—Carnival—now has a nonsmoking ship. Smoking policies vary and change; contact your cruise line to find out what the situation will be on your cruise.

Seatings

When it comes to your dining-table assignment, you should have options on four important points: early or late seating; smoking or no-smoking section (if smoking is allowed in the dining room); a table for two, four, six, or eight; and special dietary needs. When you receive your cruise documents, you will usually receive a card asking for your dining preferences. Fill this out and return it to the cruise line, but remember that you will not get your seating assignment until you board the ship. Check it out immediately, and if your request was not met, see the maître d'—usually there is a time and place set up for changes in dining assignments.

On some ships, seating times are strictly observed. Ten to 15 minutes after the scheduled mealtime, the dining-room doors are closed, although this policy is increasingly rare. On other ships, passengers may enter the dining room at their leisure, but they must be out by the end of the seating. When a ship has just one seating, passengers may enter any time the kitchen is open.

Seating assignments often apply only to dinner. Most ships have open seating for breakfast or lunch, which means you may sit anywhere at any time the meal is served. Smaller or more luxurious ships offer open seating for all meals.

Several large cruise lines now offer several restaurant and dining options and have eliminated preassigned seating, so you can dine with whom you like at any table that's available and at any time the dining room is open.

CHANGING TABLES

Dining is a focal point of the cruise experience, and your companions at meals may become your best friends on the cruise. However, if you don't enjoy the company at your table, the maître d' can usually move you to another one if the dining room isn't completely full—a tip helps. He will probably be reluctant to comply with your request after the first full day at sea, however, because the waiters, busboys, and wine steward who have been serving you up to that point won't receive their tips at the end of the cruise. Be persistent if you are truly unhappy.

Cuisine

Most ships serve food geared to the American palate, but there are also theme dinners featuring the cuisine of a particular country. Some European ships, especially smaller vessels, may offer a particular cuisine throughout the cruise—Scandinavian, German, Italian, or Greek, perhaps—depending on the ship's or the crew's nationality. The quality of cruise-ship cooking is generally good, but even a skilled chef is hard put to serve 500 or more extraordinary dinners per hour. Presentation is often spectacular, especially at gala midnight buffets.

There is often a direct relationship between the cost of a cruise and the quality of its cuisine. The food is very sophisticated on some (mostly expensive) lines, such as Crystal Cruises. In the more moderate price range, Celebrity Cruises has gained renown for the culinary stylings of French chef Michel Roux, who acts as a consultant to the line.

Special Diets

With notification well in advance, many ships can provide a kosher, low-salt, low-cholesterol, sugar-free, vegetarian, or other special menu. However, there's always a chance that the wrong dish will somehow be handed to you. Especially when it comes to soups and desserts, it's a good idea to ask about the ingredients.

Large ships usually offer an alternative "light" or "spa" menu based upon American Heart Association guidelines, using less fat, leaner cuts of meat, low-cholesterol or low-sodium preparations, smaller portions, salads, fresh-fruit desserts, and healthy garnishes. Some smaller ships may not be able to accommodate special dietary needs. Vegetarians generally have no trouble finding appropriate selections.

Wine

Wine at meals costs extra on most ships; prices are usually comparable to those in shoreside restaurants and are charged to your shipboard account. A handful of luxury vessels include both wine and liquor. On some lines, you can also select the wines you might like for dinner before leaving home and they will appear at your table and on your bill at the end of the cruise.

The Captain's Table

It is both a privilege and an interesting experience to be invited to dine at the captain's table. Although some seats are given to celebrities, repeat passengers, and passengers in the most expensive suites, other invitations are given at random to ordinary passengers. You can request an invitation from the chief steward or the hotel manager, although there is no guarantee you will be accommodated. The captain's guests always wear a suit and tie or a dress, even if the dress code for that evening is casual. On many ships, passengers may be invited to dine at the other officers' tables, or officers may visit a different passenger table each evening.

Bars

Whether adjacent to the pool or attached to a lounge, a ship's bars tend to be its social centers. Except on a handful of luxury-class ships where everything is included in the ticket price, bars operate on a pay-as-it's-poured basis. Rather than demand cash after every round, however, most ships allow you to charge drinks to an account.

In international waters there are, technically, no laws against teenage drinking, but almost all ships require passengers to be over 18 or 21 to purchase alcoholic beverages. Many cruise ships have chapters of Alcoholics Anonymous (a.k.a. "Friends of Bill W.") or will organize meetings on request. Look for meeting times and places in the daily program slipped under your cabin door each night or delivered to the cabin by the steward.

Entertainment

Lounges and Nightclubs

On ocean liners, the main entertainment lounge or show-room schedules nightly musical revues, magic acts, comedy performances, and variety shows. During the rest of the day the room is used for group activities, such as shore-excursion talks or bingo games. Generally, the larger the ship the bigger and more impressive the productions. Newer ships have elaborate showrooms that often span two decks. Some are designed like an amphitheater while others have two levels—a main floor and a balcony. Seating is sometimes in clusters of armchairs set around cocktail tables. Other ships have more traditional theater-style seating.

Many larger ships have several showrooms and a variety of bars, ranging from sports bars to piano bars and mirrored-floors-and-strobe-light dance bars. Entertainment and ball-room dancing may go late into the night; adult midnight comedy shows are popular on many ships. Elsewhere, you may find a disco, nightclub, or cabaret, usually built around a bar and dance floor. Music is provided by a piano player, a disc jockey, or by performing ensembles such as a country-and-western duo, a harpist and violinist, or a jazz combo.

On smaller ships the entertainment options are more limited, sometimes consisting of no more than a piano around which passengers gather. There may be a main lounge where scaled-down revues are staged. Often talented crew members double as entertainers, and on many ships a crew night, featuring crew members' performing dances and songs of their native lands, is a highlight.

Library

Most cruise ships have a library with up to 1,500 volumes, from the latest best-sellers to reference works. Many shipboard libraries also stock videotapes for those cabins with VCRs.

Movie Theaters

Most vessels have a room for screening movies. On older ships and some newer ones, this is often a genuine cinema-style movie theater, while on other ships it may be just a multipurpose room. Films are frequently one or two months past their first release date but not yet available on videotape or cable TV. Films rated "R" are edited to minimize sex and violence. Over the course of a weeklong voyage a dozen films may be screened, each repeated several times. Theaters are also used for lectures, religious services, and private meetings.

With a few exceptions, ocean liners equip their cabins with closed-circuit TVs showing movies (continuously on some newer ships), shipboard lectures, and regular programs (thanks to satellite reception). Ships with in-cabin VCRs usually provide a selection of movies on videocassette at no charge (a deposit is sometimes required).

Casinos

Once a ship is 12 mi off American shores, it is in international waters and gambling is permitted. (Some "cruises to nowhere," in fact, are little more than sailing casinos.) Almost all ocean liners—except Disney Cruise Line ships—as well as many cruise yachts and motor-sailing ships have casinos. On larger vessels you'll usually find poker, baccarat, blackjack, roulette, craps, and slot machines. House stakes are much more modest than those in Las Vegas or Atlantic City. On most ships the maximum bet is $200; some ships allow $500. Payouts on the slot machines (some of which take as little as a nickel) are generally much lower, too. Credit is never extended, but many casinos have handy ATM machines that dispense cash for a hefty fee.

Children are officially barred from the casinos, but it's not uncommon to see them playing the slots rather than the adjacent video machines. Most ships offer free individual instruction and off-hours gambling classes. Casinos are usually open from early morning to late night, although you may find only unattended slot machines before evening. In adherence to local laws, casinos are always closed while a ship is in port.

Game Rooms

Most ships have a game or card room with card tables and board games. These rooms are for serious players and are often the setting for friendly round-robin competitions and tournaments. Most ships furnish everything for free (cards, chips, games, and so forth), but a few charge $1 or more for each deck of cards. Be aware that professional cardsharps and hustlers have been fleecing ship passengers almost as long as there have been ships. There are small video arcades on most medium and large ships. Family-oriented ships often have a computer learning center as well.

Bingo and Other Games

The daily high-stakes bingo games are even more popular than the casinos. You can play for as little as a dollar a card. Most ships have a snowball bingo game with a jackpot that grows throughout the cruise into hundreds or even thousands of dollars. Another popular cruise pastime is so-called "horse races": fictional horses are auctioned off to "owners." Individual passengers can buy a horse or form "syndicates." Bids usually begin at around $25 and can top $1,000 per horse. Races are then "run" according to dice throws or computer-generated random numbers. Audience members bet on their favorites.

Sports and Fitness

Swimming Pools

All but the smallest ships have at least one pool, some of them elaborate affairs with water slides or retractable roofs; hot tubs and whirlpools are quite common. Pools may be filled with fresh water or saltwater; some ships have one of each. Many are too narrow or too short to allow swimmers more than a few strokes in any direction; none have diving boards, and not all are heated. Often there are no lifeguards.

Outdoor pools are usually closed on Alaskan cruises, except for those equipped with retractable roofs. Outdoor hot tubs, however, do stay in use in Alaska.

Sundeck

The top deck is usually called the Sundeck or Sports Deck. On some ships this is where you'll find the pool or whirlpool; on others it is dedicated to volleyball, basketball, table tennis, shuffleboard, and other cruise-ship sports. A number of ships have paddle-tennis courts, and a few have golf driving ranges. Often, after the sun goes down, the Sundeck is used for social activities such as barbecues and dancing under the stars.

Promenade Deck

Many vessels designate certain decks for fitness walks and may post the number of laps per mile. Fitness instructors sometimes lead daily walks around the Promenade Deck. A number of ships discourage jogging and running on the decks or ask that no one take fitness walks before 8 AM or after 10 PM, so as not to disturb passengers in cabins. With the advent of the megaship, walking and jogging have in many cases moved up top to tracks on the Sundeck or Sports Deck.

Exercise and Fitness Rooms

Most newer ships and some older ones have well-equipped fitness centers, and some have full-fledged spas, with elaborate exercise equipment, massage, sauna, whirlpools, and a wide range of spa treatments, from high-pressure water treatments to mud treatments. An upper-deck fitness center often has an airy and sunny view of the sea; an inside, lower-deck health club is often dark and small unless it is equipped with an indoor pool or beauty salon.

Many ships have full-service exercise rooms with elaborate bodybuilding and cardiovascular equipment, aerobics classes, and individual fitness instruction. Some ships offer cruise-length physical-fitness programs, which may include lectures on weight loss or nutrition. These often are tied in with a spa menu. The more extensive programs are often sold on a daily or weekly basis. There is a charge for each of the spa treatments but no charge to use the exercise equipment or attend the exercise classes.

Shipboard Services

Room Service

A small number of ships have no room service at all, except when the ship's doctor orders it for an ailing passenger. Many offer only breakfast (Continental on some, full on others); most, however, have selections that you can order around the clock, although menus may be abbreviated at some hours. Many ships now offer unlimited round-the-clock room service. There usually is no additional charge other than for beer, wine, or spirits delivered to your room.

Minibars

An increasing number of cruise lines equip cabins with small refrigerators or minibars stocked with snacks, soda, beer, wine, and liquors. There is usually a small charge for these items, just as there would be in a hotel.

Laundry and Dry Cleaning

All but the smallest ships and shortest cruises offer laundry services—full-service, coin-operated self-service, or both. Use of machines is generally free, although some ships charge for detergent, use of the machines, or both. Valet laundry service includes cabin pickup and delivery and usually takes 24 hours. Some ships also offer dry-cleaning services, but a concern for the environmental effect of the chemicals used in dry-cleaning is beginning to limit those services, so don't count on it.

Hair Stylists

Even the smallest ships have a hair stylist on staff. Larger ships have complete beauty salons, and some have barbershops. Book your appointment well in advance, especially before popular events such as the farewell dinner.

Film Processing

Many ships offer overnight film processing. It's expensive but convenient.

Photographer

The staff photographer, a near-universal fixture on cruise ships, records every memorable, photogenic moment both on board and on shore. The thousands of photos snapped over the course of a cruise are displayed publicly in special cases every morning and are offered for sale, usually for $6 to $8 for a 5″ × 7″ color print or $12 to $15 for an 8″ × 10″. If you want a special photo or a portrait, the photographer is usually happy to oblige. Many passengers choose to have a formal portrait taken before the captain's farewell dinner—the dressiest event of the cruise. The ship's photographer usually anticipates this demand by setting up a studio with an attractive backdrop near the dining-room entrance.

Religious Services

Most ships provide nondenominational religious services on Sundays and religious holidays, and some offer Catholic masses daily and Jewish services on Friday evenings. The kind of service held depends upon the clergy the cruise line invites on board. You'll often find religious services in the library, the theater, or one of the private lounges, although a few ships have actual chapels—and some offer a wedding chapel and full wedding services. Travel agents and the ship's staff can provide details.

Communications

SHIPBOARD

Most cabins have loudspeakers and telephones. Generally, the loudspeakers cannot be switched off because they are used for broadcast of important notices. Telephones are used to call fellow passengers, order room service, summon a doctor, request a wake-up call, or speak with the ship's officers or departments.

SHIP TO SHORE

Sending e-mails can be an expensive proposition, with ships charging anywhere from 50¢ to $1 a minute for Internet access. You may also purchase a package with a one-time activation fee ranging from $3.95 to $10.95. Most cruise lines offer several plans that include blocks of time—either 100 minutes ranging from $55 to $75 or 250 minutes for $100 to $150. Norwegian Cruise Lines ships are among those with wireless Internet capability, and you may bring along your own laptop with a wi-fi card or rent a laptop from the ship; you generally pay for a block of time or pay a fee for unlimited access.

Satellite facilities make it possible to call anywhere in the world from most ships. Most are also equipped with fax machines, and some provide credit-card-operated phones. It may take as long as a half hour to make a connection, but unless a storm is raging outside, conversation is clear and easy. On older ships, voice calls must be put through on shortwave wireless or via the one phone in the radio room. Newer ships are generally equipped with direct-dial phones in every cabin for calls to shore. Be warned: the cost of communication, regardless of the method, can be quite expensive—up to $15 a minute. (On some ships, though, it's much cheaper, costing as little as $3.95 a minute.) If possible, wait until you go ashore to call home. Cell phones can be used on ships, although reception depends on your distance from shore and whether your cell phone provider has service to the area where you are cruising. Many cell phones do not work outside of the United States.

SAFETY AT SEA

Once you've settled into your cabin, locate the life vests and review the emergency instructions inside the cabin door or near the life vests. Let the ship's purser know if you have a disability that may hamper a speedy exit from your cabin. In case of a real emergency, the purser can quickly dispatch a crew member to assist you. Learn to secure the vests properly. If you are traveling with children, be sure that child-size life jackets are placed in your cabin.

Within 24 hours of embarkation, you will be asked to attend a mandatory lifeboat drill. Do so and listen carefully. If you have any questions, ask them. Only in the most extreme circumstances will you need to abandon ship—but it has happened. The time you spend learning the right procedure may serve you well in a mishap.

Fire Safety

The greatest danger facing cruise-ship passengers is fire. All of the ships reviewed in this book must meet certain international fire-safety standards requiring that ships have sprinkler systems, smoke detectors, and other safety features. These rules are designed to protect against loss of life, but they do not guarantee that a fire will not happen; in fact, fire is relatively common on cruise ships. The point here is not to alarm but to emphasize the importance of taking fire safety seriously.

Health Care

Quality medical care at sea is another important safety issue. All big ships are equipped with medical infirmaries to handle minor emergencies. However, these should not be confused with hospitals. There are no international standards governing medical facilities or personnel aboard cruise ships, although the American Medical Association has recommended that such standards be adopted. If you have a preexisting medical condition, discuss your upcoming cruise with your doctor. Pack an extra supply of any medicines you might need. Once aboard, see the ship's doctor and alert him or her to your condition, and discuss treatments or emergency procedures before any problem arises. Passengers with potentially life-threatening conditions should consider signing up with a medical evacuation service, and all passengers should review their health insurance to make sure they are covered while on a cruise.

If you become seriously ill or injured and happen to be near a major city, you may be taken to a medical facility shoreside. But if you're farther afield, you may have to be airlifted off the ship by helicopter and flown either to the nearest American territory or to an airport where you can be taken by charter jet to the United States. Many standard health insurance policies, including Medicare plans, do not cover these or other medical expenses incurred outside the United States. You can, however, buy supplemental health insurance that is in effect only when you travel.

The most common minor medical problems confronting cruise passengers are seasickness and gastrointestinal distress. Modern cruise ships, unlike their transatlantic predecessors, are relatively motion-free vessels outfitted with computer-controlled stabilizers, and they usually sail in relatively calm waters. If you do feel queasy, you can get seasickness pills aboard ship. (Many ships give them out free at the front desk.)

Outbreaks of food poisoning occasionally occur aboard cruise ships. Episodes are random; they can occur on ships old and new, big and small, budget and luxury. The Centers for Disease Control and Prevention (CDC) monitors cruise-ship hygiene and sanitation procedures, conducting voluntary inspections twice a year of all ships that sail regularly from U.S. ports (this program does not include ships that never visit the United States). A high score on the CDC report doesn't mean you won't get sick. Outbreaks have taken place on ships that consistently score very highly; conversely, some ships score very poorly yet passengers never get sick.

For a free listing of the latest cruise-ship sanitation scores, write to the CDC's **National Center for Environmental Health** (Vessel Sanitation Program, 1015 North America Way, Room 107, Miami, FL 33132, tel. 888/232–3299 for fax-back service, www.cdc.gov). If you use the fax-back service, request publication 510051.

Crime on Ships

Crime aboard cruise ships has occasionally become headline news, thanks in large part to a few well-publicized cases. Most people never have any type of problem, but you should exercise the same precautions aboard ship that you would at home. Keep your valuables out of sight—on big ships virtually every cabin has a small safe in the closet. Don't carry too much cash ashore, use your credit card whenever possible, and keep your money in a secure place, such as a front pocket that's harder to pick. Single women traveling with friends should stick together, especially when returning to their cabins late at night. Be careful about whom you befriend, as you would anywhere, whether it's a fellow passenger or a member of the crew. Don't be paranoid, but do be prudent.

GOING ASHORE

Traveling by cruise ship presents an opportunity to visit many places in a short time. The flip side is that your stay in each port of call will be brief. For this reason cruise lines offer shore excursions, which maximize passengers' time. There are a number of advantages to shore excursions arranged by your ship: in some destinations, transportation may be unreliable, and a ship-packaged tour is the best way to see distant sights. Also, you don't have to worry about missing the ship. The disadvantage of a shore excursion is the cost—you pay more for the convenience of having the ship do the legwork for you. Of course, you can always book a tour independently, hire a taxi, or use foot power to explore on your own. Most of the towns have hiking trails easily accessible to port areas, and a stop at the local visitor center can help you plan a walking tour within your time limit. However, be sure to carry along rain gear and drinking water, even for the most leisurely stroll. The weather in Alaska is very fickle and subject to rapid changes.

Many of the busier port cities tend to have several ships in port at a time, and the more popular shore trips can fill up quickly. If your heart is set on a particular experience, book it before your cruise or on board as soon as you can. Some excursions, such as flightseeing trips and the Skagway narrow-gauge rail trip, are in very high demand. Information on local tours is available at the visitor-information counter usually close to the pier in each port.

Arriving in Port

When your ship arrives in a port, it will either tie up alongside a dock or anchor out in a harbor. If the ship is docked, passengers walk down the gangway to go ashore. Docking makes it easy to go back and forth between the shore and the ship.

Tendering

If your ship anchors in the harbor, you will have to take a small boat—called a launch or tender—to get ashore. Tendering is a nuisance. Passengers wishing to disembark may be required to gather in a public room, get sequenced boarding passes, and wait until their numbers are called. The ride to shore may take as long as 20 minutes. If you don't like waiting, plan to go ashore an hour or so after the ship drops its anchor.

Because tenders can be difficult to board, passengers with mobility problems may not be able to visit certain ports. The larger ships are more likely to use tenders. It is usually possible to learn before booking a cruise whether the ship will dock or anchor at its ports of call.

Before anyone is allowed to walk down the gangway or board a tender, the ship must be cleared for landing. Immigration and customs officials board the vessel to examine passports and sort through red tape. It may be more than an hour before you're allowed ashore. You will be issued a boarding pass, which you'll need to get back on board.

Returning to the Ship

Cruise lines are strict about sailing times, which are posted at the gangway and elsewhere and announced in the daily schedule of activities. Be sure to be back on board at least a half hour before the announced sailing time or you may be stranded. If you are on a shore excursion that was sold by the cruise line, however, the captain will wait for your group before casting off. That is one reason many passengers prefer ship-packaged tours.

If you're not on one of the ship's tours and the ship sails without you, immediately contact the cruise line's port representative, whose phone number is often listed on the daily schedule of activities. You may be able to hitch a ride on a pilot boat, although that is unlikely. Passengers who miss the boat must pay their own way to the next port.

2 Cruising in Alaska

ALASKA, IT WOULD SEEM, was made for cruising. The traditional route to the state is by sea, through a 1,000-mi-long protected waterway known as the Inside Passage. From Vancouver in the south to Skagway in the north, it winds around islands large and small, past glacier-carved fjords and hemlock-blanketed mountains. This great land is home to breaching whales, nesting eagles, spawning salmon, and calving glaciers. The towns here can be reached only by air or sea; there are no roads between them. Juneau, in fact, is the only water-locked state capital in the United States. Beyond the Inside Passage, the Gulf of Alaska leads to Prince William Sound—famous for its marine life and more fjords and glaciers—and Anchorage, Alaska's largest city.

Alaska is one of cruising's showcase destinations, so the lines are sailing their grandest ships in these waters. Itineraries give passengers more choices than ever before—from traditional loop cruises of the Inside Passage, round-trips from Vancouver, Seattle, or San Francisco, to one-way Inside Passage–Gulf of Alaska cruises. A few smaller boats sail only in Prince William Sound, away from big-ship traffic.

Following the latest trend in cruising, more and more families are setting sail for Alaska. The peak season falls during summer school vacation, when children are a common sight aboard ship. Cruise lines have responded with programs designed specifically for children and with some discount shore excursions for youngsters under 12. Shore excursions have become more active, too, often incorporating activities families can enjoy together, such as bicycling, kayaking, and hiking.

For adults, too, the cruise lines now offer more than ever before. Most lines have pre- or post-cruise land tours as an optional part of a package trip, and onboard entertainment and learning programs are extensive. Some lines hire celebrity or native speakers, naturalists, or local personalities to lead discussions stimulated by the local environment.

Dining is an important part of the cruise experience, and that's where many of the lines are putting their efforts.

Cruise-ship cuisine is varied and plentiful: casual fare is available all day, and most large ships offer 24-hour room service. The food served in the dining rooms and onboard restaurants is easily on par with that of the best urban eateries. Traditionally, cruise-ship passengers are assigned a table and a sitting for dinner and dine at the same time, with the same companions and waitstaff, each evening. Some cruise lines maintain this custom, while others are adding a variety of onboard restaurants and allowing passengers to dine when, where, and with whom they like.

Many of the larger ships now also boast extensive fitness centers and spas, as well as a varied menu of evening entertainment that can include anything from recent movies to Las Vega–style revues. Despite these bells and whistles, though, the highlight of any Alaska cruise is bound to be the natural wonder of the land itself.

CHOOSING YOUR CRUISE

Every ship has its own personality, depending on its size, the year it was built, and its intended purpose. Each type satisfies a certain type of passenger, and for every big-ship fan there is someone who would never set foot aboard one of these "floating resorts."

The type of ship you choose is the most important factor in your Alaska cruise vacation, because it will determine how you see Alaska. Ocean liners sail farther from land and visit major ports of call such as Juneau, Skagway, and Ketchikan. These big ships are more stable and offer a huge variety of activities and facilities. Small ships spend much of their time hugging the coastline, looking for wildlife, waterfalls, and other natural and scenic attractions. They feel intimate, like private clubs.

Luxury ships are not your only option for traveling to Alaska. There are a few rugged expedition-type vessels, and for more independent types, there's no better way to see Alaska than aboard the ferries of the Alaska Marine Highway System, which allow you to travel with your car or RV and explore at your own pace.

Types of Ships

Ocean Liners

Alaska's ocean-liner fleet represents the very best that today's cruise industry has to offer. Nearly all the ships were built within the last two decades and have atrium lobbies, state-of-the-art health spas, high-tech show lounges, elaborate dining rooms, and a variety of alternative restaurants. They are a comfortable and sometimes even luxurious way to tour Alaska's major ports of call and scenic attractions. By night they come alive with Vegas-style revues, pulsating discos, and somewhat more sedate cabaret or comedy acts. Most of the latest liners have cabins with verandas—a great bonus in Alaska for watching the scenery go by from the privacy of your own stateroom. The newest cruise ships are lined with glass throughout their corridors and public rooms, so you're never far from the sea or a great view.

Small Ships

Unlike ocean liners, the smaller vessels cruising in Alaska are designed to reach into the most remote corners of the world. Shallow drafts allow them to navigate up rivers, close to coastlines, and into shallow coves. Hulls may be hardened for sailing in Arctic ice. Motorized rubber landing craft, known as Zodiacs, are usually kept on board, making it possible for passengers to put ashore almost anywhere. However, because the emphasis aboard smaller ships tends to be on learning and exploring, the ships don't have casinos, shows, multiple bars and lounges, and other typical diversions. Instead, for entertainment they have onboard libraries and enrichment programs led by experts.

With just a few dozen passengers, smaller vessels are more homey and intimate than the larger liners and offer plenty of opportunity for the passengers and crew to get to know one another.

Ferries

The state ferry system is known as the Alaska Marine Highway because its vessels carry vehicles as well as passengers. Each ferry has a car deck that can accommodate every size vehicle from the family car to a Winnebago. This capability presents an opportunity for independent travelers with wanderlust: you can take your vehicle ashore, drive around, even live in it, and then transport it with you to the next port of call. From Skagway or Haines (the only Inside Passage towns connected to a road system), you can drive farther north to Fairbanks and Anchorage by way of the Alaska Highway. Each ferry also has a main, or "weather," deck to accommodate passengers, and on-board camping is allowed year-round. You can start your voyage as far south as Bellingham, Washington, or Prince Rupert, British Columbia, both of which are ports of call for Alaskan Marine Highway ferries. You can also sail north on British Columbia Ferries from Port Hardy, B.C., to Prince Rupert, B.C., and pick up an Alaska ferry from there.

Itineraries

You'll want to give some consideration to your ship's Alaskan itinerary when you are choosing your cruise. The length of the cruise will determine the variety and number of ports you visit, but so will the type of itinerary and the point of departure. **Loop cruises** start and end at the same point and usually explore ports close to one another; **one-way cruises** start at one point and end at another and range farther afield.

Ocean liners typically follow one of two itineraries: round-trip Inside Passage loops starting and finishing in Vancouver, B.C., or Seattle; and one-way Inside Passage–Gulf of Alaska cruises sailing between Vancouver or Seattle and Anchorage. Both itineraries are usually seven days, though some lines offer longer trips. A few lines also schedule one-way or round-trip sailings from San Francisco or Los Angeles. Small ships typically sail within Alaska, setting out from Juneau, Sitka, or other Alaskan ports.

Whether you sail through the Inside Passage or along it will depend on the size of your vessel. Smaller ships can navigate narrow channels, straits, and fjords. Larger vessels must sail farther from land, so don't expect to see much wildlife from the deck of a megaship.

Cruise Tours
Most cruise lines give you the option of an independent, hosted, or fully escorted land tour before or after your cruise. Independent tours allow maximum flexibility. You

have a preplanned itinerary with confirmed hotel reservations and transportation arrangements, but you're free to follow your interests and whims in each town. A hosted tour is similar, but tour-company representatives are available along the route to help out should you need assistance. On fully escorted tours, you travel with a group, led by a tour director. Activities are preplanned (and typically prepaid), so you have a good idea of how much your trip will cost (not counting incidentals) before you depart.

Most cruise-tour itineraries include a ride aboard the Alaska Railroad in a glass-dome railcar. Running between Anchorage, Denali National Park and Preserve, and Fairbanks are Holland America Westours' *McKinley Explorer,* Princess Tours' *Midnight Sun Express,* and the Royal Caribbean *Wilderness Express,* which offer unobstructed views of the passing land and wildlife from private railcars. If you choose to travel by rail independently, the Alaska Railroad cars are clean and comfortable and make the trip between Anchorage and Fairbanks hooked up to the same engines as the cruise-line cars.

Also popular among cruise passengers is independent travel by rental car or RV before or after the cruise segment. Generally passengers will plan to begin or end their cruise in Anchorage, the most practical port city to use as a base for exploring the state. Almost any type of car or recreational vehicle, from a small, two-person RV to a large, luxurious motor home, can be rented, and there are few restrictions on where you can park it to spend the night.

Of the ocean-liner fleets, only Carnival Cruise Lines, Crystal Cruises, Norwegian Cruise Lines, and World Explorer Cruises are not currently offering cruise-tour packages with land segments in Alaska; they may, however, have tours in the Canadian Rockies. In addition to full-length cruise tours, many cruise lines have pre- or post-cruise hotel and sightseeing packages in Vancouver, Seattle, or Anchorage lasting one to three days.

Cruise Costs

Cruise costs can vary enormously. If you shop around and book early you will undoubtedly pay less. Your cruise fare typically includes accommodation and all onboard meals, snacks, and activities. It does not normally include airfare to the port city, shore excursions, tips, alcoholic drinks, or spa treatments. Only the most expensive Alaska cruises include airfare. Virtually all lines offer air add-ons, which may or may not be less expensive than the latest discounted fare from the airlines.

Shore excursions can be a substantial expense; the best in Alaska are not cheap. But, skimp too much on your excursion budget and you'll deprive yourself of an important part of the Alaska experience.

Tipping is another extra. At the end of the cruise, it's customary to tip your room steward, server, and the person who buses your table, though some lines include the tips in the fare. If tips are not included, expect to pay an average of $7.50 to $10 per day in tips. Each ship offers guidelines.

Single travelers should be aware that there are few single cabins on most ships; taking a double cabin for yourself can cost as much as twice the advertised per-person rates (which are based on two people sharing a room). Some cruise lines will find roommates of the same sex for singles so that each can travel at the regular per-person, double-occupancy rate.

When to Go

Cruise season runs from mid-May to late September; the most popular sailing dates are from late June through August. Although Alaskan weather never carries any guarantees, sunshine and warm days are apt to be most plentiful from mid-June through August. May and June are the driest months to cruise. Bargains can be found both early and late in the season.

Cruising in the low seasons provides plenty of advantages besides discounted fares. Availability of ships and particular cabins is greater in the low and shoulder seasons, and the ports are almost completely free of tourists. In spring, wildflowers are abundant, and you're apt to see more wildlife along the shore because the animals have not yet gone up to higher elevations. Alaska's early fall brings the splendor of autumn hues and the first snowfalls in the mountains. The animals have returned to low ground, and shorter days bring the possibility of seeing the northern lights. Daytime temperatures along the cruise routes in May, June, and September are in the 50s and 60s. July and August averages are in the 60s and 70s, with occasional days in the 80s.

November is the best month for off-season ferry travel, after the stormy month of October and while it's still relatively warm on the Inside Passage (temperatures will average about 40°F). It's a good month for wildlife watching as well. Some animals show themselves in greater numbers during November. In particular, humpback whales are abundant off Sitka, and bald eagles congregate by the thousands near Haines.

OCEAN LINERS

For each cruise line, we list only the ships (grouped by similar configurations) that regularly cruise in Alaska. When two or more ships are substantially similar, their names are given at the beginning of a review and separated by commas. The ships for each cruise line are listed in order from largest to smallest.

Passenger-capacity figures are given on the basis of two people sharing a cabin (basis-2); however, many of the larger ships have 3- and 4-berth cabins, which can increase the total number of passengers tremendously when all berths are occupied. When total occupancy figures differ from basis-2 occupancy, we give them in parentheses.

Luxury Cruise Lines

The ultra-luxury cruise lines, which in Alaska include Crystal and Seven Seas, offer high staff-to-guest ratios for personal service, superior cuisine, and a highly inclusive product with few onboard charges. These small and midsize ships offer much more space per passenger than you will find on the mainstream lines' vessels.

If you consider travel an entitlement rather than a luxury and frequent exclusive resorts, then you will appreciate the extra attention and the higher level of comfort that these luxury cruise lines can offer.

Crystal Cruise Line

Crystal's two mid-sized ships stand out for their modern design, amenities, and spaciousness. The vessels were built to deliver the first-rate service of a luxurious, small ship, but they have many of the onboard facilities of a big ship. Crystal ships have long set standards for onboard pampering. White-glove service, stellar cuisine, and even air-conditioned tenders complete the effect of total luxury and comfort. To the typical litany of ocean-liner diversions, Crystal adds destination-oriented lectures and talks by scholars, political figures, and diplomats, plus luxe theme cruises emphasizing such topics as food and wine or the arts.

Crystal's target clientele is affluent and older but still active. On select cruises highly trained and experienced youth counselors are brought in to oversee activities for kids and teens. Staff are well trained, friendly, highly motivated, and thoroughly professional. However, alone among the luxury lines, Crystal's fares do not include tips, so the crew can be noticeably solicitous of gratuities. The line's casinos are operated by Caesars Palace at Sea.

Suggested tipping guidelines are as follows: stewardess, $4 per day (single travelers, $5 per day); waiter, $4 per day ($6 per day in alternative restaurants); assistant waiter, $2.50 per day; butler penthouse, $4 per day; 15% added to bar bills. Tips for other personnel are at your discretion. Gratuities may be charged to a shipboard account.

Crystal Cruise Line, 2049 Century Park E, Suite 1400, Los Angeles, CA 90067, tel. 800/446–6620 or 310/785–9300, fax 310/785–9201, www.crystalcruises.com.

THE SHIPS OF CRYSTAL CRUISE LINE

Ⓢ **Crystal Harmony.** The only Alaska-bound liner offering 12-day round-trip sailings from San Francisco, Crystal's sleek ship is uncluttered, with classy, understated interiors. *Harmony* has plenty of open deck space for watching the scenery, and the forward observation lounge, set high above the bridge, has oversize windows. Best of all, it is roomy, with one of the highest ratios of passenger to space of any ship. Staterooms deliver space in abundance—the smallest measuring 183 square ft—and more than half have private verandas. Even the lowest-category staterooms have a separate sitting area (love seat with coffee table), a desk/vanity, and queen or twin beds—with space left over to move about comfortably. Large closets, ample drawer space, and bathtubs are standard. Cabins are equipped with voice mail, goose-down pillows, fine linens, and thick towels. Onboard amenities include grand lounges and Broadway-style entertainment. *408 cabins, 940 passengers, 8 passenger decks. Dining room, 2 restaurants, café, grill, ice cream parlor, in-room safes, minibars, in-room VCRs, 2 pools, 1 lap pool, fitness classes, gym, hair salon, 2 outdoor hot tubs, sauna, spa, steam room, 7 bars, casino, cinema, dance club, showroom, video game room, children's program (ages 3–16), dry cleaning, laundry facilities, laundry service, computer room, Internet, no-smoking rooms; no kids under 3 months.*

Seven Seas Cruises

Seven Seas Cruises (formerly Radisson Seven Seas Cruises) is part of Carlson Hospitality Worldwide, one of the world's major hotel and travel companies. The cruise line was formed in December 1994 with the merger of the one-ship Diamond Cruises and Seven Seas Cruises lines. From these modest beginnings, SSC has now grown into a major luxury player in the cruise industry. With the launch of the line's fifth ship, the *Seven Seas Mariner* in March 2001, SSC became the world's largest luxury line, with more than 2,000 berths in this category.

The line's spacious, ocean-view cabins have the industry's highest percentage of private balconies; you'll always find open seating at dinner (which includes complimentary wine); there's a strict no-tipping policy; and activities tend to be oriented toward exploring the destinations on the itinerary. Although passengers tend to be older and affluent they are still active, and SSC manages to provide a high level of service and sense of intimacy on mid-sized ships, which have the stability of larger vessels.

Seven Seas Cruises, 600 Corporate Dr., Suite 410, Fort Lauderdale, FL 33334, tel. 954/776–6123, 800/477–7500, or 800/285–1835, fax 954/772–3763, www.rssc.com.

THE SHIPS OF SEVEN SEAS CRUISES

Seven Seas Mariner. The world's first and only all-suite, all-balcony ship is also Radisson Seven Seas' largest, with the highest space-per-passenger ratio in the fleet. All cabins are outside suites ranging from 301 square ft to 1,580 square ft, including the veranda. The ship's dining rooms include Signatures, the only restaurant at sea staffed by chefs wearing the Blue Riband of Le Cordon Bleu of Paris, the famed culinary institute. On certain voyages the chefs offer Le Cordon Bleu "Classe Culinaire des Croisiers," workshops that offer a hands-on introduction to the art of French cooking. Passengers on SSC ships have consistently placed the Judith Jackson spas among their favorites on land or sea. *328 cabins, 700 passengers, 8 passenger decks. Dining room, 3 restaurants, in-room safes, minibars, in-room VCRs, pool, fitness classes, gym, hair salon, outdoor hot tub, sauna, spa, steam room, 4 bars, casino, cinema, dance club, showroom, children's programs (ages 6–17), dry cleaning, laundry service, no-smoking rooms; no kids under 1.*

Mainstream Cruise Lines

Generally speaking, the mainstream lines have two sizes of ship—cruise liner and megaship—in their fleets. Cruise liners have plentiful outdoor deck space, and most have a wraparound outdoor promenade deck that allows you to stroll or jog the ship's perimeter. In the newest cruise liners, traditional meets trendy. You find atrium lobbies and expansive sundecks and sports decks, picture windows instead of portholes, and cabins that open onto private verandas. The smallest cruise liners carry 500 passengers, while the largest accommodate 1,500 passengers and are stuffed with diversions.

The centerpiece of most megaships is a three-, five-, or seven-story central atrium. However, these giant vessels are most easily recognized by their profile: the hull and superstructure rise as many as 14 stories out of the water and are capped by a huge sundeck or sports deck with a jogging track. Some megaships have a wraparound promenade deck. Picture windows are standard equipment, and cabins in the top categories have private verandas. From their casinos and discos to their fitness centers, everything is bigger and more extravagant than on other ships. If you're into big, bold, brassy, and nonstop activity, these huge ships offer it all. You may want to rethink a cruise aboard one of these ships if you want a little downtime, however, since you'll be joined by 1,500 to 3,000 fellow passengers.

Carnival Cruise Lines

Carnival Cruise Lines is the largest and most successful cruise line in the world, carrying more passengers than any other. Today's Carnival is a vastly different company from the one launched in 1972 with one refitted transatlantic ocean liner by entrepreneur Ted Arison, who made a vacation experience once reserved for the very rich widely accessible. Carnival became the standard by which lower-priced cruise lines are measured. Not even its critics can deny that the line delivers what it promises. Brash and sometimes rowdy, Carnival throws a great party. Activities and entertainment are nonstop, beginning just after sunrise and continuing well into the night. Food has been upgraded in recent years, and it is plentiful and fairly diverse, better tasting and well presented, with healthy options.

Cabins are spacious and comfortable, comparable with those on any ship in this price category. Carnival's ships are like floating theme parks, though each one has a personality. The effect is most exaggerated on the newer, bigger ships, including the Fantasy, Destiny, Spirit, and Conquest classes. The *Carnival Conquest,* the largest, at 110,000 tons, debuted in November 2002; other megaships will be added to the fleet through 2005.

Carnival cruises are popular with young, single cruisers as well as with those older than 55. The line's offerings also appeal to parents cruising with their children. Dinner in the main dining room is served at 6 PM and 8 PM seatings. While Carnival's "Total Choice Dining" is not really a meal plan, all ships serve food at all hours, including 24-hour room service.

Gratuities are customarily given on the last evening of the cruise, but they may be prepaid at a rate of $9.75 per passenger per day. Carnival recommends the following tips: cabin steward, $3.50 per day; dining-room team service, $5.50 per day; alternative dining service, 75¢ per day. A 15% gratuity is automatically added to bar and beverage tabs.

Carnival Cruise Lines, 3655 N.W. 87th Ave., Miami, FL 33178-2428, tel. 305/599–2600, 800/438–6744, or 800/327–9501, www.carnival.com.

THE SHIPS OF CARNIVAL CRUISE LINES

☝ *Spirit.* The first of Carnival's Spirit-class ships entered service in 2001 with notable design improvements over previous lines. For example, all staterooms aboard these superliners are located above ocean level, making for a more comfortable cruise. Cabins have ample drawer and closet space, and in-cabin TVs show first-run films. Other innovations include eye-popping 11-story atriums, two-level promenades (partially glass-enclosed to create a protected viewing perch), wide decks, shopping malls, and reservations-only supper clubs. Greater speed allows Spirit-class ships to visit destinations in a week that would take other ships 10 days or more. Most staterooms have ocean views, and of those 80% have balconies. Terrific children's programs and a pool with a retractable roof for all-weather swimming make this a good ship for any family vacation. *1,062 cabins, 2,124 passengers (2,667 at full occupancy), 13 passenger decks. Dining room, 3 restaurants, pizzeria, in-room safes, 4 pools, fitness classes, gym, hair salon, 5 outdoor hot tubs, spa, 16 bars, casino, cinema, dance club, showroom, video game room, children's programs (ages 2–15), laundry facilities, laundry service, computer room, no-smoking rooms.*

Celebrity Cruises

Celebrity Cruises has made a name for itself based on sleek ships and superior food. Style and layout vary from ship to ship, lending each a distinct personality. In terms of size and amenities, Celebrity's vessels rival almost any in cruising, but with a level of refinement rare on bigger ships. In just a short time Celebrity has won the admiration of its passengers and its competitors—who have copied its occasional adults-only cruises, nouvelle cuisine, and cigar clubs and hired its personnel (a true compliment). Celebrity has risen above typical mass-market cruise cuisine by hiring chef Michel Roux as a consultant. Menus are creative;

both familiar and exotic dishes have been customized to appeal to American palates. All food is prepared from scratch, using only fresh produce and herbs, aged beef, and fresh fish—even the ice cream on board is homemade. Entertainment choices range from Broadway-style productions, captivating shows, and lively discos to Monte Carlo–style casinos and specialty lounges.

Celebrity attracts everyone from older couples to honeymooners. Summertime children's programs are as good as those on any upscale cruise line. Service is friendly and first class—rapid and accurate in the dining rooms. Waiters, stewards, and bartenders are enthusiastic, take pride in their work, and try to please.

Tip your cabin steward/butler $3.50 per day, chief housekeeper 50¢ per day, dining-room waiter $3.50 per day, assistant waiter $2 per day, and restaurant manager 75¢ per day, for a total of $10.25 per day. A 15% service charge is added to all beverage checks. For children under 12, or the third or fourth person in the stateroom, half of the above amounts is recommended. Gratuities are typically handed out on the last night of the cruise, or they may be charged to your shipboard account.

Celebrity Cruises, 1050 Caribbean Way, Miami, FL 33132-2096, tel. 305/539–6000 or 800/646–1456, fax 800/437–5111, www.celebritycruises.com.

THE SHIPS OF CELEBRITY CRUISES

Infinity, Summit. Dramatic exterior glass elevators, a glass-domed pool area, and a window-wrapped ship-top observation lounge keep the magnificence of Alaska well within the passenger's view aboard these Millennium-class ships. These are the newest and largest in Celebrity's fleet, and each stocks plenty of premium amenities, including a flower-filled conservatory, music library, expansive spa, Internet café with 18 work stations, golf simulator, and brand-name boutiques. Cabins are bright, spacious, and well appointed, and 80% have an ocean view (74% of those have private verandas). There is also Internet access in some cabins. With a staff member for every two passengers, service is especially attentive. *975 cabins, 1,950 passengers, 11 passenger decks. Dining room, restaurant, food court, ice cream parlor, pizzeria, in-room safes, minibars, in-room VCRs, 3 pools, fitness classes, gym, hair salon, 3 outdoor hot tubs, sauna, spa, steam room, 6 bars, casino, cinema, dance club, showroom, video game room, children's programs (ages 3–17), dry cleaning, laundry service, computer room, no-smoking rooms.*

⏱ **Mercury.** With features such as a golf simulator, video walls, and interactive television systems in cabins, this ship is a high-tech pioneer yet at the same time it is elegant and warm. Many large windows—including a dramatic two-story wall of glass in the dining room and wraparound windows in the Stratosphere Lounge, in the gym, and in the beauty salon—bathe the ship in natural light and afford excellent views of Alaska's natural beauty. Plus there are retractable glass sunroofs over the pools. The elaborate Elemis spas have enormous Thalassotherapy pools and the latest in treatments. Standard cabins are intelligently appointed and apportioned, with few frills; space is well used, making for maximum elbow room in the bathrooms and good storage space in the closets. *935 cabins, 1,870 passengers, 10 passenger decks. Dining room, 2 restaurants, food court, ice cream parlor, pizzeria, in-room safes, minibars, 3 pools, fitness classes, gym, hair salon, 4 outdoor hot tubs, sauna, spa, steam room, 6 bars, casino, cinema, dance club, showroom, video game room, children's programs (ages 3–17), dry cleaning, laundry service, computer room, no-smoking rooms.*

Holland America Line

Founded in 1873, Holland America (HAL) is one of the oldest names in cruising. Steeped in the traditions of the transatlantic crossing, its cruises are classic, conservative affairs renowned for their grace and gentility. The line falls at the high end of the premium category and is deluxe by any standard. Service is taken seriously: the line maintains a school in Indonesia to train staff members rather than hiring out of a union hall. The staff on the line's Alaska cruises includes a naturalist and native artist-in-residence, who are on hand to offer instruction in the region's history and wildlife. Food is good by cruise-ship standards and served on Rosenthal china. In response to the challenge presented by its competitors, Holland America has gone "nouvelle" and introduced a lighter side to its menus, including many pastas and "heart-healthy" dishes. Holland America passengers tend to be older and less active than those traveling on the ships of its parent line, Carnival, although the age difference is getting narrower. As its ships attract a more youthful clientele, Holland America has taken steps to shed its "old folks" image, now offering trendier cuisine and a "Club Hal" children's program. Still, these are not party cruises, and Holland America has managed to preserve the refined and relaxing qualities that have always been its hallmark.

Between 2003 and 2006, Holland America is expected to launch three additional 85,000-ton Vista-class ships, including the *Oosterdam*, which will sail to Alaska in 2004.

In the 1970s, Holland America adopted a no-tips-required policy. Staff members perform their duties with great pride and professionalism. In turn, passengers don't feel the pressure or the discomfort of having crew members solicit tips. On the other hand, this is not a no-tipping policy, and most passengers give tips comparable to those recommended on other lines—entirely at their own discretion.

Holland America Line, 300 Elliott Ave., Seattle, WA 98119, tel. 206/281–3535 or 877/932–4259, fax 206/281–7110, www.hollandamerica.com.

THE SHIPS OF HOLLAND AMERICA LINE

☙ *Oosterdam.* Panoramic views from exterior elevators are a dramatic addition to this new Vista-class ship. Launched in 2003, the *Oosterdam* boasts more space per passenger—in both public rooms and cabins—than any other ship in the Holland America fleet. All the HAL trademarks, including lush traditional decor, white-gloved stewards, and a multimillion-dollar art collection, are here, as are such up-to-date touches as in-cabin Internet access, a golf simulator, extensive spa facilities, and an alternative restaurant with a Pacific Northwest menu. A retractable dome over the pool means you can enjoy a swim, even in Alaska. *924 cabins, 1,848 passengers, 11 decks. Dining room, 2 restaurants, café, some in-room VCRs, 3 pools, fitness classes, gym, hair salon, sauna, spa, 4 bars, casino, cinema, dance club, showroom, children's programs (ages 5–17), dry-cleaning, laundry service, computer room, Internet, no-smoking rooms*

♻ *Volendam, Zaandam.* These ships are structurally similar to HAL's other vessels, with the signature two-tier dining room and retractable roof over the main pool, but they are newer, entering service in 1999 and 2000, respectively. They are also slightly larger than the line's other ships and have Internet cafés and practice-size tennis courts. Priceless antiques and artwork line the halls; huge bouquets of fresh, fragrant flowers are everywhere (a Holland America trademark); and each ship has a teak promenade completely encircling the ship, which means there will always be room for you at the rail to watch the sunset. All standard outside cabins come with a bathtub, and all suites and minisuites have private verandas. The "Passport to Fitness" encourages a healthy diet and exercise. *658/720 cabins (Volendam/Zaandam), 1,316/1,440 passengers (1,378/1,848 at full occupancy), 10/10 passenger decks. Dining room, 2 restaurants, food court, in-room safes, refrigerators, in-room VCRs, 2 pools (1 indoor), fitness classes, gym, hair salon, 2 outdoor hot tubs, sauna, spa, steam room, 6 bars, casino, cinema, dance club, showroom, video game room, children's programs (ages 5–17), dry cleaning, laundry facilities, laundry service, computer room, Internet, no-smoking rooms.*

Amsterdam. Holland America Lines is known for its old-world elegance, and the *Amsterdam* delivers with antiques, original art, brass fixtures, and teak deck chairs. It is a new ship, however, with such up-to-date amenities as practice-size tennis courts, a pool with a retractable roof, and an Internet café. The promenade, which completely encircles the ship, ensures plenty of viewing space. *690 cabins, 1,380 passengers, 10 decks. Dining room, 2 restaurants, café, pool, fitness classes, gym, hair salon, hot tub, sauna, spa, 6 bars, casino, dance club, showroom, children's programs (ages 5–17), dry cleaning, laundry facilities, laundry service, computer room, Internet.*

Maasdam, Ryndam, Statendam, Veendam. An abundance of glass, outdoor deck space, and a retractable roof over the main pool make these good ships for Alaska cruising. Great views can be found along the wraparound promenade. From bow to stern, these ships are full of lounges and restaurants—14 in all—some cozy, some grand, and most with expansive floor-to-ceiling windows. The Crow's Nest is a combined observation lounge and nightclub overlooking the bow, and the Lido Restaurant, the hallmark of every Holland America Line ship, has an adjoining outdoor terrace. A three-deck atrium and a two-tier dining room, replete with dual grand staircases framing an orchestra balcony, are among the welcoming public spaces. Antiques and artwork line the halls; staterooms are restful, with understated elegance. *633 cabins, 1,266 passengers (1,590 at full occupancy), 10 passenger decks. Dining room, 3 restaurants, food court, ice cream parlor, in-room safes, 2 pools, fitness classes, gym, hair salon, 2 hot tubs, sauna, spa, steam room, 9 bars, casino, cinema, dance club, showroom, video game room, children's programs (ages 5–17), dry cleaning, laundry facilities, laundry service, computer room, Internet, no-smoking rooms.*

Prinsendam. Teak decks, antiques, and specially commissioned artworks grace Holland America's smallest vessel. New to Alaska in 2003, the *Prinsendam* offers a high crew-to-passenger ratio and a more intimate feel than some of the newer megaships. The cabins are roomy, and 40% have private verandas. *398 cabins, 793 passengers (837 full occupancy), 9 decks. Dining room, 2 restaurants, café, 2 pools, fitness classes, gym, hair salon, hot tub, sauna, spa, 4 bars, casino, dance club, showroom, children's programs (ages 5–17), dry cleaning, laundry facilities, laundry service, computer room, Internet, no-smoking rooms.*

Norwegian Cruise Line

Norwegian Cruise Line (NCL) was established in 1966, when one of Norway's oldest shipping companies, Oslo-based Klosters Rederi A/S, acquired the *Sunward* and launched a new concept in cruising: regularly scheduled cruises on a single-class ship. No longer simply a means of transportation, the ship became a destination unto itself, an affordable alternative to land-based resorts. NCL continues to innovate. As Princess did with its Personal Choice concept, NCL offers "Freestyle Cruising," which eliminates dinner-table and -time assignments and dress codes. The line has even loosened the rules on disembarkation, which means passengers can relax in their cabins until it's time to leave the ship (instead of gathering in a lounge to wait for their numbers to be called).

Most of NCL's Alaska fleet is based in Seattle rather than Vancouver, which can be a more convenient departure point for many U.S.-based passengers. The line's passenger list usually includes senior citizens, families, and younger couples, mostly from the United States and Canada.

NCL applies a service charge to passengers' shipboard accounts: $10 per passenger per day for those 13 and older and $5 per day for children ages 3–12. These automatic tips can be increased, decreased, or removed. A 15% gratuity is added to bar tabs and spa bills.

Norwegian Cruise Line, 7665 Corporate Center Dr., Miami, FL 33126, tel. 305/436–4000 or 800/327–7030, www.ncl.com.

THE SHIPS OF NORWEGIAN CRUISE LINE

☼ **Norwegian Star.** NCL's newest and, at 25 knots, its fastest, Alaska-bound ship was built specifically to accommodate the line's "Freestyle Cruising" concept. Offering more dining choices than any other ship in Alaska, *Star* has 10 different eateries, with everything from French, Italian, and spa cuisine to tapas, sushi, and Pacific Rim fusion. The ship also has a two-deck, 24-hour fitness center; a Balinese-themed spa; a golf driving range; and an indoor pool. Garden Villas, the top-of-the-line staterooms, have private rooftop terraces. Standard cabins take their cue from high-end hotel rooms, with rich cherry wood, tea and coffee makers, and large bathrooms. Most staterooms can accommodate a third guest, and many cabins can be linked to create suites for larger groups. *1,120 cabins, 2,240 passengers, 11 passenger decks. 2 dining rooms, 6 restaurants, 2 cafés, food court, ice cream parlor, in-room safes, refrigerators, 2 pools (1 indoor), fitness classes, gym, hair salon, 2 hot tubs, spa, 9 bars, cinema, 2 dance clubs, showroom, video game room, children's programs (ages 2–17), dry cleaning, laundry service, computer room, Internet.*

☼ **Norwegian Sky, Norwegian Sun.** These ships come with all the bells and whistles, including a variety of dining options, specialty bars, and Internet access—both in a café and in cabins. A 24-hour health club has expansive ocean views, and the presence of the full-service Mandara Spa means you can turn your cruise into a spa vacation. Cabins are adequately laid out, with large circular windows and sitting areas, sufficient (but not generous) shelf and drawer space, and two lower beds that convert to a queen. But what makes Norwegian Cruise Line's ship different from other large ships is its relaxed onboard atmosphere and Free-Style Dining concept, which means main dining rooms are smaller but there are more dining venues (some with an additional cost). *1,001/1,001 cabins (Sky/Sun), 2,002/2,002 passengers (2,400/2,400 full occupancy), 12/11 passenger decks. 2 dining rooms, 8/7 restaurants, food court, in-room safes, refrigerators, 2 pools, fitness classes, gym, hair salon, 4 hot tubs, sauna, spa, steam room, 13/11 bars, casino, cinema, dance club, showroom, video game room, children's programs (ages 2–17), dry cleaning, laundry facilities, computer room, Internet; no kids under 6 months.*

Princess Cruise Line

Rising from modest beginnings in 1965, when it began with one ship cruising to Mexico, Princess has become one of the world's largest cruise lines. Its fleet goes to more destinations each year than any other major line, and many cruises depart from the West Coast of the United States. Princess was catapulted to stardom in 1977, when it became the star of *The Love Boat* television series, which introduced millions of viewers to the still-new concept of a seagoing vacation. The name and famous "seawitch" logo have remained synonymous with cruising ever since. Nearly everything about Princess is big, but the line doesn't sacrifice quality for quantity when it comes to building beautiful vessels. Service, especially in the dining rooms, is of a high standard. In short, Princess is refined without being pretentious.

Many Princess ships offer the line's innovative "Personal Choice Cruising" program, an individualized, unstructured style of cruising that gives passengers choice and flexibility in customizing their cruise experience—multiple dining locations, flexible entertainment, and affordable private balconies. It's the kind of program that has become important for the entire industry.

Princess passengers' average age is 45; you see a mix of younger and older couples on board.

Princess suggests tipping $10 per person, per day. On ships with Personal Choice Cruising gratuities are automatically added to accounts, which passengers can adjust at the purser's desk; 15% is added to bar bills.

Princess Cruise Line, 24305 Town Center Dr., Santa Clarita, CA 91355-4999, tel. 661/753-0000 or 800/774-6237, www.princess.com.

THE SHIPS OF PRINCESS CRUISE LINE

Coral Princess, Island Princess. Launched in 2003, these sister ships offer a wealth of high-tech amenities. The two-story Universe Lounge has full TV production capabilities and three revolving stages; the wedding chapel is complete with video cameras; plus there's an Internet café and a golf simulator. Also on board are a 9-hole putting green, a 60s-theme martini bar, and a Cajun-style restaurant with live jazz. The retractable dome roof on the pool allows for all-weather swimming. Ninety percent of cabins are outside staterooms, and most of those have balconies. Princess's "Personal Choice Cruising" allows you to choose between traditional fixed seating in the dining room or dining when you like in any of the onboard restaurants. *987 cabins, 1,970 passengers,11 passenger decks. 2 dining rooms, 2 restaurants, 2 cafés, ice cream parlor, pizzeria, in-room safes, 4 pools, fitness classes, gym, hair salon, 5 hot tubs, sauna, spa, 5 bars, casino, cinema, dance club, 3 showrooms, video game room, children's programs (ages 3–17), dry cleaning, laundry facilities, laundry service, computer room, Internet; no kids under 6 months.*

Sun Princess, Dawn Princess. More than 70% of outside cabins in these sister ships have private balconies. All standard cabins are decorated in light colors and have a queen-size bed convertible to two singles, ample closet and bath space (with shower only), terry robes, and hair dryers. Several cabins on each ship are deemed fully accessible. A wraparound teak promenade lined with canopied steamer chairs provides a peaceful setting for reading, napping, or daydreaming, while a pool with a retractable glass roof allows for all-weather swimming. *975 cabins, 1,950 passengers, 14 passenger decks. 5 restaurants, 3 dining rooms, café, food court, ice cream parlor, pizzeria, in-room safes,* *refrigerators, 5 pools, fitness classes, gym, hair salon, 9 hot tubs, sauna, spa, steam room, 12 bars, casino, cinema, dance club, showroom, video game room, children's programs (ages 3–17), dry cleaning, laundry facilities, laundry service, computer room, no-smoking rooms; no kids under 6 months.*

Royal Caribbean Cruise Line

Imagine if the Mall of America were sent to sea. That's a fair approximation of what the megaships of Royal Caribbean Cruise Line (RCL) are all about. These giant vessels are indoor-outdoor wonders, with every conceivable activity in a resort-like atmosphere, including atrium lobbies, shopping arcades, large spas, and expansive sundecks. Several ships have such elaborate facilities as 18-hole miniature-golf courses, ice-skating rinks, and rock-climbing walls. These mammoth ships are quickly replacing the smaller vessels in Royal Caribbean's fleet, and passengers now have three generations of megaships to choose from, including the prototype, the *Sovereign of the Seas.*

The centerpiece of Royal Caribbean's megaships is the central atrium, a hallmark that has been duplicated by many other cruise lines. The brilliance of this design is that all the major public rooms radiate from this central point, so you can learn your way around these huge ships within minutes of boarding. Ships in the Vision series (*Legend of the Seas* and *Vision of the Seas*) are especially big and airy, with sea views almost anywhere you happen to be. The main problem with its otherwise well-conceived vessels is that the line packs too many people aboard, making for an exasperating experience at embarkation, while tendering, and at disembarkation. However, Royal Caribbean is one of the best-run and most popular cruise lines.

While the line competes directly with Carnival for passengers—active couples and singles in their thirties to fifties, as well as a large family contingent—there are distinct differences of ambience and energy. Royal Caribbean is a bit more sophisticated and subdued than Carnival, even while delivering a good time on a grand scale.

Royal Caribbean suggests the following tips per passenger. Dining room waiter, $3.50 a day; stateroom attendant,

$3.50 a day, assistant waiter, $2 a day. Gratuities for head-waiters and other service personnel are at your discretion. A 15% gratuity is automatically added to beverage and bar bills. All gratuities may be charged to your onboard account.

Royal Caribbean International, 1050 Caribbean Way, Miami, FL 33132, tel. 305/539–600 or 800/327–6700, www.royalcaribbean.com.

THE SHIPS OF ROYAL CARIBBEAN CRUISE LINE

🐧 *Radiance of the Seas.* Speed (which allows for longer itineraries) and the line's highest percentage of outside cabins are the selling points here. More than 80% of all cabins have ocean views, and more than 70% of those include private verandas. All cabins have two twin beds convertible into a queen, computer jack, vanity table with an extendable working surface, and bedside reading lights. The central atrium spans 10 decks, and sea-facing elevators give you a view of the ocean. The coffeehouse-bookstore combination, the rock-climbing wall, and the self-leveling pool tables are novel touches. The African-theme solarium, with its retractable glass roof, pool, hot tubs, palm trees, and waterfalls, provides a pleasant escape from inclement Alaskan weather. *1,056 cabins, 2,100 passengers (2,501 full occupancy), 12 passenger decks. 3 dining rooms, 5 restaurants, food court, in-room data ports, in-room safes, refrigerators, 3 pools, fitness classes, gym, hair salon, 3 hot tubs, sauna, spa, steam room, 9 bars, casino, cinema, dance club, showroom, video game room, children's programs (ages 3–17), dry cleaning, laundry service, computer room, no-smoking rooms.*

Legend of the Seas, Vision of the Seas. These sister ships are among the fastest on the Alaska run. Both have large windows throughout and, on the uppermost deck, a viewing lounge with wraparound glass. The covered pool and indoor-outdoor deck area of the Solarium Spa are especially well suited to cruising in often rainy Alaska. Among the bright, spacious cabins are connecting staterooms, cabins with private balconies, and family suites with separate bedrooms for parents and children. *900/1200 cabins (Legend/Vision), 1,800/2,400 passengers, 9/10 passenger decks. Dining rooms, 2 restaurants, 2 pools, fitness classes, gym, hair salon, 4/6 hot tubs, sauna, spa, steam room, 8/6& bars, casino, dance club, showroom, children's programs (ages 3–17), computer room, Internet.*

SMALL SHIPS

Compact expedition-type vessels bring you right up to the shoreline to skirt the face of a glacier and pull through narrow channels where big ships don't fit. Alaska, not casinos or spa treatments, is the focus of these cruises. You'll see more wildlife and call into smaller ports, as well as some of the larger, better-known towns. Lectures and talks—conducted daily by naturalists, Native Alaskans, and other experts in the Great Land's natural history and native cultures are the norm. But in comparison with those on the ocean liners, cabins on expedition ships can be quite tiny, usually with no phone or TV, and some bathrooms are no bigger than cubbyholes. Often, the dining room and the lounge are the only common public areas on these vessels. Other small ships, however, are luxurious yachts with cushy cabins, comfy lounges and libraries, and hot tubs on deck. You won't find discos or movie theaters aboard, but what you trade for space is a unique and detailed glimpse of Alaska that you're unlikely to forget.

The ships for each cruise line are listed in order from largest to smallest. When two or more ships are substantially similar, their names are given at the beginning of a review and separated by commas.

American Safari Cruises

"Luxury in pursuit of adventure" is the tagline for this high-end yacht-cruise line, which operates some of the smallest vessels in Alaska. Unlike most other yachts, which have to be chartered, American Safari's vessels sail on a regular schedule and sell tickets to individuals: there's no need to charter the whole boat, though that is an option. With just 12 to 21 passengers and such decadent amenities as ocean-view hot tubs, American Safari's yachts are among the most comfortable small ships cruising Alaska. The chefs serve fine Pacific Northwest cuisine with plenty of local seafood, a choice of individually prepared dinner entrées, and breads and desserts made fresh on board.

Shallow drafts mean these little ships and their landing craft can reach hidden inlets and remote beaches and slip in for close-up looks at glaciers and wildlife. Itineraries are usually flexible; there's no rush to move on if the group spots a pod of whales or a family of bears. All sailing is in daylight, with nights spent at anchor in secluded coves, and the yachts stop daily to let you kayak, hike, or beachcomb. An onboard naturalist offers informal lectures and guides you on shore expeditions. All three ships carry exercise equipment, kayaks, mountain bikes, Zodiac landing crafts, and insulated Mustang suits for Zodiac excursions.

Quest makes weeklong sailings between Juneau and Sitka. *Escape* and *Spirit* offer eight-night cruises between Juneau and Prince Rupert, B.C. In May or September, there are the 15-day repositioning cruises between Seattle and Juneau.

All shore excursions—even a flightseeing trip—and alcoholic drinks are included in the fare. Tips are discretionary, but 5% to 10% of the fare is suggested. A lump sum is pooled among the crew at the end of the cruise.

American Safari Cruises, 19101 36th Ave. W, Suite 201, Lynnwood, WA 98036, tel. 425/776–4700 or 888/862–8881, fax 425/776–8889, www.amsafari.com.

THE SHIPS OF AMERICAN SAFARI CRUISES

Safari Quest. American Safari's largest vessel, this luxurious yacht has warm wood trim throughout. Four cabins have small balconies accessed by sliding glass doors, and a single cabin is available. There's plenty of outer deck space for taking in the views, and a reading lounge on the top deck is a pleasant hideaway. *11 cabins, 21 passengers, 4 passenger decks. Dining room, in-room VCRs, outdoor hot tub, bar; no smoking.*

Safari Spirit. A comfortable lounge and an open bar are part of the pampering, as are the excellent meals, served at one grand table. Every bright and cheerful cabin has a private bath with a hot tub; the high-end cabins have king beds; and one has a small balcony. *6 cabins, 12 passengers, 4 decks. Dining room, in-room VCRs, outdoor hot tub, bar; no smoking.*

Safari Escape. Although *Escape* is one of Alaska's smallest cruise ships, it comes with all kinds of creature comforts usually associated with bigger ships, including exercise equipment, mountain bikes, and, in one cabin, a private sauna. Everyone dines together at one grand table; lunch might be a gourmet picnic on a secluded beach. Standard staterooms have queen or twin beds and port lights rather than windows. The higher-end staterooms have a king-size bed and a window. All have rich fabrics and wood paneling. *6 cabins, 12 passengers, 3 passenger decks. Dining room, in-room VCRs, outdoor hot tub, bar; no smoking.*

American West Steamboat Company

In the 19th century, paddle wheelers were a key part of Alaska's coastal transport, taking adventurers and gold seekers north. In 2003, American West Steamboat Company launched the *Empress of the North*, the first overnight stern-wheeler to ply these waters in 100 years. This faithful re-creation recalls the grand coastal paddle wheelers of the past, from the lavish decor to the stern-wheeler powering the ship.

The *Empress* has an impressive collection of Alaskan art and historic artifacts on board, and a naturalist and historian gives lectures on local history and culture. Gold-rush follies, Russian-American dances, and Native American songs and dances bring the region's past to life.

In 2004, the *Empress* will make eight-night round-trip sailings from Sitka, with stops at the Southeast's major ports and visits to Glacier Bay and Tracy Arm. A shore excursion is included at each port of call, including a trip on the White Pass and Yukon Railroad. This novel small ship is expected to attract primarily North American passengers, with an average age of about 55.

As with most small ships, tips are pooled by the crew at the end of cruise. A tip of $12 to $14 per person per night is suggested.

American West Steamboat Company, 2101 4th Ave., Suite 1150, Seattle, WA 98121, tel. 206/621–0913 or 800/434–1232, fax 206/340–0975, www.americanweststeamboat.com.

THE SHIPS OF AMERICAN WEST STEAMBOAT COMPANY

Empress of the North. Alaskan art and historical artifacts enrich the public areas, and the staterooms mimic Victorian opulence, with lush fabrics and rich colors. All cabins have big picture windows, and most have balconies. Lavish two-room suites, as well as single, triple, and wheelchair-accessible cabins are available. The chandelier-lit dining room looks formal, but it is actually small-ship casual, with open seating and no need to dress up. Variety shows, ranging from golden oldies and big band to country-and-western, play nightly. *112 cabins, 235 passengers, 4 passenger decks. Dining room, café, minibars, in-room DVDs, 3 bars, showroom; no smoking.*

Clipper Cruise Lines

Clipper Cruise Lines keeps the focus on fully experiencing each destination. A fleet of motorized Zodiacs is on hand to take passengers to isolated beaches, and on every voyage, onboard experts share their knowledge of the region's cultures, wildlife, history, and geography. Occasionally, local musicians and artists will join the ship at ports of call, and crew members are enthusiastic young Americans.

Clipper chefs take pride in their healthy American cuisine. Each dish is made to order, and almost everything served is made from scratch on board. There are a number of choices at each meal, including light selections and half portions. You can take your time over dinner, as there's only one sitting in the dining room.

There's little formality on board these relaxed yacht-size cruisers. Casual attire is the norm, and sports coats and dresses don't usually appear until the captain's farewell party. Passengers are typically active and well-traveled older adults.

The Clipper Odyssey makes 13-day journeys between Anchorage and Prince Rupert, B.C.; 9-day sailings round-trip from Prince Rupert to Juneau; and 14-day cruises from Anchorage across the Bering Sea to Russia. *The Yorktown Clipper* makes 8-day sailings between Juneau and Ketchikan. In May and September, 12-day cruises between Seattle and Juneau explore the folklore and natural history of the whole Inside Passage.

Tips are pooled together at the end of the cruise. Ten dollars per day per passenger is suggested.

Clipper Cruise Lines, 11969 Westline Industrial Dr., St. Louis, MO 63146-3220, tel. 314/655–6700 or 800/325–0010, www.clippercruise.com.

THE SHIPS OF CLIPPER CRUISE LINES

Yorktown Clipper. Although deck space is limited on this coastal cruiser, floor-to-ceiling windows in the forward observation lounge and large windows in the dining room allow sightseeing in all weather. Cabins are all outside, with twin lower berths, and a private bathroom with a shower. Most have large windows. *69 cabins, 138 passengers, 4 passenger decks. Dining room, in-room safes, bar; no smoking.*

Clipper Odyssey. The *Odyssey* brings elements of a luxury yacht experience to small-ship cruising in Alaska. Window-lined dining rooms and lounges keep the scenery in sight. Each cabin also has an ocean view, as well as a sitting area with a sofa and a bathroom with a shower and tub. Other amenities include exercise equipment, a jogging track, and a library. *64 cabins, 128 passengers, 5 passenger decks. Dining room, in-room safes, refrigerators, gym, hair salon, outdoor hot tub, bar, laundry service; no smoking.*

Cruise West

A big player in small ships, the Seattle-based Cruise West sends seven coastal cruisers to Alaska each summer. As with other smaller vessels, Alaskan wilderness, wildlife, and culture take precedence over shipboard diversions. Ports of call include small fishing villages and native settlements as well as major towns. An exploration leader, who is both naturalist and cruise coordinator, offers evening lectures and joins passengers on many of the shore excursions—at least one of which is included at each port of call. At some stops, local guides come on board to add their insights, and schedules are flexible to make the most of wildlife sightings. Binoculars in every cabin, a library stocked with books of local interest, and crew members as keen to explore Alaska as the passengers all enhance the experience.

Cruise West is family-owned, and this is reflected in the ships' homey atmosphere. The lounge feels like a living room; wholesome meals include bread baked on board; and jeans are as formal as it gets. The passengers, who inevitably get to know one another during the cruise, are typically active, well-traveled over-fifties. They come from all regions of the United States, as well as from Australia, Canada, and the United Kingdom.

The fleet travels the Inside Passage between Seattle and Juneau and between Vancouver, B.C., and Anchorage. Other options include cruises along Alaska's Inside Passage, sailings in Prince William Sound, and voyages across the Bering Sea to Russia. There is also a daylight yacht tour aboard the *Sheltered Seas,* during which you cruise by day and stay in a shoreside hotel each night. Land tours can be added to most of these itineraries.

Suggested tips are $10 per person per day; these are pooled for all the crew and staff at the end of the cruise.

Cruise West, 2401 4th Ave., Suite 700, Seattle, WA 98121, tel. 206/441–8687 or 800/888–9378, www.cruisewest.com.

THE SHIPS OF CRUISE WEST

Spirit of Oceanus. Cruise West's largest vessel is also its most luxurious, with marble and polished wood in the dining room, lounges, library, and cabins. All the staterooms are outside, and 12 of them have teak-floor private balconies. The ship, equipped with stabilizers for open ocean cruising, also carries a fleet of Zodiacs for close-up visits to glaciers, waterfalls, and icebergs. Breakfast and lunch are served on deck when the weather permits. *57 cabins, 114 passengers, 5 decks. Dining room, in-room safes, refrigerators, in-room VCRs, gym, outdoor hot tub, bar; no smoking.*

Spirit of Endeavour. One of Cruise West's largest and fastest ships, the *Endeavour* provides ample deck space and a roomy lounge with large picture windows for superb views. Most of the cabins also have picture windows, and some have connecting doors, which make them convenient for families traveling together. The ship's speed allows for more flexibility: the captain can linger to let passengers watch a group of whales, and still make the next stop on time. Exercise equipment is available. *51 cabins, 102 passengers, 4 passenger decks. Dining room, some refrigerators, in-room VCRs, bar; no smoking.*

Spirit of '98. With rounded stern and wheelhouse, old-fashioned smokestack, and Victorian decor, the *Spirit of '98* evokes a turn-of-the-20th-century steamer, although she is actually a modern ship, built in 1984. Mahogany trim inside and out, overstuffed chairs with plush floral upholstery, and a player piano in the salon add to the gold-rush-era motif. For private moments, you'll find plenty of nooks and crannies aboard the ship, including the cozy Soapy's Parlor bar at the stern. All cabins, including the two single cabins on board, have picture windows. The Owner's Suite has a living room and a whirlpool tub. Exercise equipment is available. *48 cabins, 96 passengers, 4 passenger decks. Dining room, some refrigerators, in-room VCRs, bar; no smoking.*

Spirit of Discovery. Floor-to-ceiling windows in the main lounge provide stunning views aboard this snazzy cruiser. From here, passengers have direct access to a large outdoor viewing deck, one of two aboard. Every cabin has windows; toilets and showers are a combined unit. Two cabins are reserved for single travelers, and exercise equipment is available on board. *43 cabins, 84 passengers, 3 decks. Dining room, some refrigerators, some in-room VCRs, bar; no smoking.*

Spirit of Alaska. The sleek *Spirit of Alaska* carries a fleet of Zodiacs for impromptu stops at isolated beaches and close-up looks at glaciers. Most cabins are small but cheerfully decorated. Toilets and showers are a combined unit (the toilet is inside the shower). Top deck cabins have windows on two sides, so you can sample both port and starboard views. Solo travelers can book a lower deck cabin with no single supplement. Exercise equipment is available. *39 cabins, 78 passengers, 4 passenger decks. Dining room, some refrigerators, some in-room VCRs, bar; no smoking, no TV in some rooms.*

Spirit of Columbia. The *Columbia*'s interior is inspired by the national park lodges of the American West, with muted shades of evergreen, rust, and sand. Cabins range from windowless inside units (which solo travelers can book with no single supplement) to comfortable staterooms with chairs and picture windows. The Columbia Deluxe cabin stretches the width of the vessel; just under the bridge, its row of forward-facing windows gives a captain's-eye view of the ship's progress. Exercise equipment is available on board. *39 cabins, 78 passengers, 4 passenger decks. Dining room, some refrigerators, some in-room VCRs, bar; no smoking.*

Sheltered Seas. Passengers on this daylight touring yacht cruise the Inside Passage by day and spend each night ashore at hotels at Ketchikan, Petersburg, and Juneau. The *Sheltered Seas* has all the amenities of other small ships, including full meal service, an onboard naturalist, lounges on two levels, and large viewing decks both fore and aft. This unique style of cruising is popular with Alaskan residents and with visitors who like a chance to see coastal towns when other visitors have returned to their ships for the night. *No cabins, 70 passengers, 2 passenger decks. Dining room, bar; no smoking.*

Glacier Bay Cruiseline

Owned in part by Tlingit people, descendants of those who settled the Glacier Bay area thousands of years ago, this cruise line has something of an inside scoop on the history, culture, and wildlife of the great land. The ships' greatest assets are the naturalists who lead shore walks and kayak excursions. They get as much of a thrill as the passengers do whenever wildlife is sighted. Glacier Bay's ships, dubbed Sport Utility Vessels, are designed for soft-adventure cruising. Each has a fleet of kayaks, a floating kayak launch, and landing craft to take passengers ashore for beachcombing and hiking expeditions.

Fleece and outdoor gear, not jackets and ties, are the norm on board, and the small group quickly grows to feel like a family (or perhaps a team on the more adventurous trips). Food is hearty and home-style. Vegetarian choices are always available, and special diets can be accommodated with advance notice.

Glacier Bay offers three different cruise styles: Low, Medium and High Adventure. Low Adventure cruises, which focus on scenic cruising and port calls, include a 10-day Inside Passage itinerary that takes in the sights and the better-known ports of call between Seattle and Juneau. Medium Adventure trips—typically eight-day itineraries within Alaska—alternate days of cruising, landing craft excursions and port visits with days of moderate-intensity hiking and kayaking. The six-day High Adventure voyages appeal to serious outdoor enthusiasts. These itineraries bypass towns altogether and take passengers on hiking and kayaking trips in remote areas each day of the cruise. These trips start with a flight from Juneau to Glacier Bay (airfare is extra).

All itineraries include at least one night at anchor in Glacier Bay and at least one shore excursion at each port. Add-ons include stays at Glacier Bay Lodge, the only overnight accommodation in Glacier Bay National Park. This phone- and TV-free cedar lodge sits on the edge of a sheltered cove, backed by mountains. The 56 rooms are connected by a boardwalk to the main lodge, which is also the National Park Service headquarters. Park Service rangers lead daily walks directly from the lodge.

Glacier Bay cruises attract active, adventurous 30- to 60-year-olds, though, of course, the High Adventure cruises call for a greater level of physical fitness than the Low Adventure trips. Adventure gear and training are included in the fare, and single supplements are waived in May and September.

Tipping is discretionary, but $15 to $20 per person per day is suggested. Tips are pooled among the staff and crew at the end of the cruise.

Glacier Bay Cruiseline, 107 W Denny Way, Suite 303 Seattle, WA 98119, tel. 206/623–2417 or 800/451–5952, www.glacierbaycruiseline.com.

THE SHIPS OF GLACIER BAY CRUISELINE

Wilderness Discoverer. Glacier Bay's large ship has plenty of viewing space on two decks. The surroundings are simple and decorated with Alaskan art. Most cabins have picture windows, and several can accommodate three passengers. Four outside staterooms on the top deck have queen beds and large picture windows. Only the pricier cabins have TVs, but there is a communal TV and VCR in the main lounge. *44 cabins, 96 passengers, 4 passenger decks. Dining room, some in-room VCRs, bar; no smoking, no TV in some rooms.*

Wilderness Adventurer. This friendly ship has the casual comforts of home. The coffee's always on and you'll never need a jacket and tie for dinner. A full wrap deck makes the most of sunny days; Alaskan art and varnished wood enhance the otherwise simple interior. Some cabins are triples. A library of books and videos has a nice selection of Alaska titles. There are no TVs, but you can watch the library tapes—or your own wildlife footage—on the VCR in the main lounge. *34 cabins, 76 passengers, 3 passenger decks. Dining room, bar; no room TVs, no smoking.*

Wilderness Explorer. The *Wilderness Explorer* is billed as a "floating base camp" for "active adventure," and that's no exaggeration. Sea-kayak outings may last more than three hours (a 5-mi paddle). Discovery hikes cross dense thickets and climb rocky creek beds. You'll spend most of your time off the ship—a good thing, since you wouldn't want to spend much time on it. The ship is pleasant enough, but it's strictly utilitarian. Public spaces are limited and the cabins are positively tiny; all but one have bunk beds. This ship should be considered only by the serious outdoor enthusiast. *16 cabins, 32 passengers, 3 passenger decks. Dining room, bar; no smoking, no room TVs.*

Lindblad Expeditions

The ships of Lindblad Expeditions forgo port calls at larger, busier towns and instead spend time looking for wildlife, exploring out-of-the way inlets, and making Zodiac landings at isolated beaches. Each ship has a video-microphone, a hydrophone, and an underwater camera so passengers can listen to whale songs and watch live video of what's going on beneath the waves. In the evening, the ships' naturalists recap the day's sights and adventures over cocktails in the lounge. A video chronicler captures the whole cruise on tape.

An eight-day expedition from Juneau to Sitka stops at such less-visited towns as Petersburg, but passengers spend most of their time spotting whales, stopping for shore walks with the ship's naturalists, exploring fjords by kayak. In May and August you can join an 11-day journey between Seattle and Glacier Bay, which includes visits to Canadian islands, native cultural centers, and artists' studios. Add-ons include a trip via coach and Alaska Railway to a lodge in Denali National Park.

Lindblad attracts active, adventurous, well-traveled over-forties, with quite a few singles, given the lines' generous singles policy.

All shore excursions except flightseeing are included, and Lindblad charges one of the industry's lowest single supplements. Tips of $12 per person per day are suggested; these are pooled among the crew at journey's end.

Lindblad Expeditions, 720 5th Ave., New York, NY 10019, tel. 212/765–7740 or 800/397–3348, www.expeditions.com.

THE SHIPS OF LINDBLAD EXPEDITIONS

Sea Bird, Sea Lion. These small, shallow-draft sister ships can tuck into nooks and crannies that big ships can't reach. An open-top sundeck, forward observation lounge, and viewing deck at the bow offer plenty of room to take in the scenery. These ships are comfortable, but public spaces and cabins are small. All staterooms are outside, but the lower-category cabins have portholes rather than windows. *37 cabins, 70 passengers, 4 passenger decks. Dining room, bar; no smoking.*

FERRY LINERS

Alaska Marine Highway System

Serving 32 ports of call in Alaska as well as Bellingham, Washington, and Prince Rupert, B.C., Alaskan ferries are a scenic option for getting to and around Alaska. Ferry travel is generally slow: maximum speed is 16.5 knots, compared with 21 knots or better for the typical large cruise ship. However, two fast ferries, the M.V. *Fairweather*, which, at press time, was due to start service between Juneau and Sitka in 2004, and the M.V. *Chenega*, planned for the Cordova, Whittier, and Valdez route in 2005, will motor at twice that speed.

Ferries are a great way to take in the landscape, meet local people, and maybe see a whale or two. The ferry system also affords freedom of movement. Unlike the big cruise ships, which follow a set itinerary, ferries come and go frequently. You can get on and off whenever you wish and stay as long as you want. Ferries serve major towns daily and call at smaller centers every two to three days, though some exotic routes, including the Cross-Gulf and Aleutian Chain ferries, see service only once a month. Stops are often made at smaller communities, such as Angoon and Tenakee Springs—just a strip of houses on stilts huddled along the shoreline. Another advantage of ferry travel is affordable fares.

The ferries are less than luxurious but comfortable enough. Each has a glass-lined observation lounge, and all but the smallest ferries have a bar. Onboard cafeterias serve hearty, inexpensive meals. Cabins are simple and serviceable, and camping in the solarium is an option. Cabins book up almost instantly for cruises during the summer season; it's essential to book in advance if you're traveling with a vehicle. A number of tour operators sell packages that include shipboard accommodations. **Knightly Tours** (Box 16366, Seattle, WA 98116, tel. 206/938–8567 or 800/426–2123, fax 206/938–8498, www.knightlytours.com) is one of the most established of these.

Alaska Marine Highway System, 6858 Glacier Hwy., Juneau, AK 99801-7909, tel. 907/465–3941 or 800/642–0066, fax 907/277–4829, www.state.ak.us/ferry.

British Columbia Ferries

British Columbia Ferries, or BC Ferries, takes vehicles and passengers from Port Hardy, on the northern tip of Vancouver Island, to Prince Rupert, B.C., where you can pick up an Alaska Ferry to continue your journey north. The ferries have cabins and cafeterias on board and the journey takes 15 hours in summer, somewhat longer in winter. Reservations are required for vehicles and recommended for foot passengers. BC Ferries also provides service to Vancouver Island from the British Columbia mainland.

1112 Fort St., Victoria, BC V8V 4V2, tel. 250/386–3431, 888/223–3779 in B.C. and Alberta only, fax 250/381–5452, www.bcferries.com.

3 Ports of Call

NEARLY EVERY DAY YOUR SHIP will make a port call, allowing you to explore the culture, wildlife, history, and amazing scenery that make Alaska so unique. Most Alaskan port cities are small and easily explored on foot, but if you prefer to be shown the sights, ship-organized shore excursions are available. Some options are bus tours, flightseeing, charter fishing, river rafting, and visits to Native communities.

Pleasures and Pastimes

Dining

Not surprisingly, seafood dominates most menus. In summer, salmon, halibut, crab, cod, and prawns are usually fresh. Restaurants are informal and casual clothes are the norm; you'll never be sent away for wearing jeans to an Alaskan restaurant.

CATEGORY	ALASKA*	VANCOUVER AND VICTORIA*
$$$$	over $25	over C$40
$$$	$16–$25	C$28–C$40
$$	$9–$15	C$15–C$27
$	under $9	under C$15

per person for a main course at dinner

Hiking and Sea Kayaking

There are hiking and walking opportunities in or near every Alaska port town. Well-maintained trails circle or branch out from even the largest cities, leading to protected forests and wilderness areas, port and glacier views, or spectacular mountaintop panoramas. More adventurous travelers will enjoy paddling sea kayaks in the protected waters of Southeast and South Central Alaska. There are companies that rent kayaks and give lessons and tours in Ketchikan, Homer, Juneau, Seward, Sitka, and Valdez, and Whittier.

Saloons

Socializing at a bar or saloon is an old Alaska custom, and the towns and cities of the Southeast Panhandle are no exception. Listed under the individual ports of call are some favorite gathering places.

Alaska Cruising Region

KENAI MTS.

Anchorage
Whittier
Seward
Valdez
Cordova

College Fjord

Prince William Sound

Mt. St. Elias

Icy Bay

Gulf of Alaska

Yakutat

GLENN HWY.

ALASKA RANGE

ALASKA HWY.

Klondike R.
Dawson

YUKON TERRITORY

Whitehorse

Carcross

Haines
Skagway

Glacier Bay National Park and Preserve

Juneau

BRITISH COLUMBIA

Sitka

Baranof Island

Inside Passage

Petersburg
Wrangell

Misty Fjords National Monument

Revillagigedo Island

Ketchikan

PACIFIC OCEAN

Prince Rupert

Peace River

Queen Charlotte Islands

Fraser R.

| 0 | | 250 miles |
| 0 | | 375 km |

Vancouver Island

KEY

⛴ Ports of Call
— Rail Lines

Vancouver

Victoria

Shopping

Alaskan Native handicrafts range from Tlingit totem poles—a few inches high to several feet tall—to Athabascan beaded slippers and fur garments. Traditional pieces of art are found in gift shops up and down the coast: Inupiat spirit masks, Yupik dolls and dance fans, Tlingit button blankets and silver jewelry, and Aleut grass baskets and carved wooden items. To ensure authenticity, buy items tagged with the state-approved AUTHENTIC NATIVE HANDCRAFT FROM ALASKA "Silverhand" label, or look for the polar bear symbol indicating products made in Alaska. Better prices are found in the more remote villages where you buy directly from the artisan, in museum shops, or in crafts fairs such as Anchorage's downtown Saturday Market.

Salmon, halibut, crab, and other seafood products are very popular souvenirs and make great gifts. Most towns have a local company that packs and ships fresh, smoked, or frozen seafood.

Anchorage

Nearly half of all Alaskans, 261,000 people, live in Anchorage, the state's only true metropolis. Superficially, Anchorage looks much like any other sprawling western American city, with Wal-Marts, espresso stands, and shopping malls, but here sled-dog racing is as popular as surfing is in California, and moose frequently roam along city bike trails. The Chugach Mountains rise around the city in a striking, spiky frame, and the spectacular Alaskan wilderness is found just out the back door. Downtown Anchorage is famous for the colorful flowers that spill from hanging baskets and window boxes all summer long.

Anchorage took shape with the construction of the federally funded Alaska Railroad completed in 1923. With the tracks laid, the town's pioneer settlers actively sought expansion by hook and—not infrequently—by crook. City founders delighted in telling how they tricked a visiting U.S. congressman into dedicating the site for a federal hospital that had not yet been approved.

Boom and bust periods followed major events: an influx of military bases during World War II; a massive buildup of Arctic missile-warning stations early in the Cold War; and the construction of the trans-Alaska pipeline with the discovery of oil at Prudhoe Bay. Nearly all the city's buildings postdate the massive 1964 earthquake—one of the largest in recorded history.

Anchorage today is Alaska at its most urban. There's a performing-arts center, a diversity of museums and shops, and scores of restaurants and brewpubs for you to sample.

Coming Ashore

Cruise ships visiting the Anchorage area most often dock at the port city of Seward, 125 mi to the south on the Kenai Peninsula; from here you travel by bus (three hours) or train (four hours) to Anchorage. The train station is a few blocks away from downtown Anchorage. Princess Cruises now stops at Whittier, on the western shore of Prince William Sound. The few ships that do sail directly to Anchorage dock just north of downtown. There is an information booth on the pier. The major attractions are best accessed by taking a taxi downtown. It is only a 15- or 20-minute walk from the dock to town, but this is through an industrial area with heavy traffic. Anchorage is the starting or ending point for many Alaskan cruises, with passengers flying into (or out of) the city. Direct rail service is available to downtown Anchorage.

TAXIS

The main tourist district of downtown Anchorage is easy to navigate on foot. If you want to see some of the outlying attractions, such as Lake Hood, you'll need to hire a taxi. Taxi rates start at $2 for pickup and $2 for each mile (2 km). Most people in Anchorage telephone for a cab, although it is possible to hail one downtown. Alaska Cab has taxis with wheelchair lifts.

Contacts **Alaska Cab** (tel. 907/563–5353, www.alaskacabs. com). **Anchorage Taxi Cab** (tel. 907/245–2207). **Borealis Shuttle** (tel. 907/276–3600 or 888/436–3600, www. borealisshuttle.com). **Checker Cab** (tel. 907/276–1234). **Yellow Cab** (tel. 907/272–2422).

RENTAL CARS

To explore sites farther afield, such as Denali, Girdwood, and points south on the Kenai Peninsula, Anchorage is the ideal place to rent a car. National Car Rental has a down-town office. Arctic Rent-a-Car, Budget, and Denali Car Rental all have airport desks and provide free shuttle service to the airport to pick up cars.

Contacts**Arctic Rent-a-Car** (tel. 907/561–2990). **Budget** (tel. 907/243–0150). **Denali Car Rental** (tel. 907/276–1230). **National Car Rental** (1300 E. 5th Ave., tel. 907/265–7553).

Exploring Anchorage
Numbers in the margin correspond to points of interest on the Downtown Anchorage map.

❶ A marker in front of the sod-roofed **Log Cabin Visitor Information Center** shows the air mileage to various world cities. Behind the cabin is a larger visitor center stocked with brochures. Fourth Avenue sustained heavy damage in the great 1964 earthquake. The businesses on this block withstood the destruction, but those a block east fell into the ground as the earth under them slid toward Ship Creek. *Corner of 4th Ave. and F St., tel. 907/274–3531, www.anchorage.net. Open June–Aug., daily 7:30–7; May and Sept., daily 8–6; Oct.–Apr., daily 9–4.*

❷ Anchorage's centerpiece is its distinctively modern **Alaska Center for the Performing Arts,** where musical, theatrical, and dance groups perform throughout the year. During the summer, IMAX films are shown inside. Out front is flower-packed **Town Square,** a delightful place to relax on a sunny day. *5th Ave. at G St., tel. 907/263–2787 or 907/263–2900, www.alaskapac.org.*

❸ The art deco **Fourth Avenue Theater** (between F and G streets) has been restored and put to use as a gift shop, café, and gallery. Note the lighted stars in the ceiling that form the Big Dipper against a field of blue—it's the design of the Alaska state flag. *630 W. 4th Ave., tel. 907/257–5600. Open daily 8–5.*

❹ Displays about Alaska's national parks, forests, and wildlife refuges can be seen at the **Alaska Public Lands Information Center.** The center also shows films highlighting different regions of the state and sells natural history books. *4th Ave. and F St., tel. 907/271–2737, www.nps.gov/aplic. Open daily 9–5:30.*

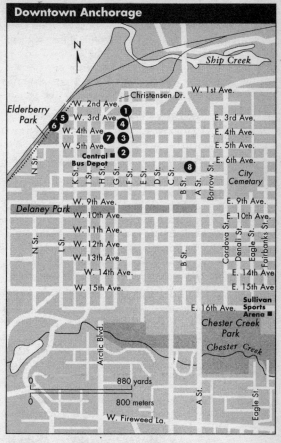

Downtown Anchorage

Alaska Center
for the
Performing
Arts 2
Alaska Public
Lands
Information
Center 4
Anchorage
Museum of
History
and Art 8

Fourth Avenue
Theater 3
Imaginarium .7
Log Cabin
Visitor
Information
Center 1

Oscar
Anderson
House
Museum 6
Resolution
Park 5

⑤ Resolution Park, a cantilevered viewing platform dominated by a monument to British explorer Captain Cook, looks out toward Cook Inlet and the mountains beyond. Mt. Susitna (locally called the Sleeping Lady) is the prominent low mountain to the northwest. To her north, Mt. McKinley is often visible 125 mi away. (Most Alaskans prefer the traditional, Native name for this peak, Denali.)

The paved **Tony Knowles Coastal Trail** runs along Cook Inlet for about 11 mi and is accessible from the west end of 2nd Avenue. This is a wonderful place to take in the view or to join the throngs of folks walking, running, biking, or skating.

⑥ The **Oscar Anderson House Museum,** next to the trail at the north end of tiny Elderberry Park, was Anchorage's first permanent frame house, built in 1915. Tours are included in your admission. In late summer the park is also a good place to watch for porpoise-size beluga whales in Cook Inlet. *420 M St., tel. 907/274–2336, www.anchoragehistoricproperties. org. Admission: $3. Open Mon.–Sat. noon–5.*

⑦ A fun stop for both children and adults is the **Imaginarium,** an interactive science museum that lets kids stand inside a giant soap bubble, hold a starfish in the marine exhibit, or take a galaxy tour in the planetarium. There's also a great gift shop. *725 W. 5th Ave., tel. 907/276–3179, www.imaginarium.org. Admission: $5. Open Mon.–Sat. 10–6, Sun. noon–5.*

⑧ The **Anchorage Museum of History and Art** occupies the entire block at 6th Avenue and A Street, with an entrance on 7th Avenue. It houses a fine collection of historical and contemporary Alaskan art, displays on Alaskan history, and a special section for children. One gallery is devoted to views of Alaska, as seen by early explorers, painters, and contemporary artists. Informative 45-minute tours are given several times a day, and the café is an excellent lunch option. *121 W. 7th Ave., tel. 907/343–4326, 907/343–6173 recorded information, www.anchoragemuseum.org. Admission: $6.50. Open Fri.–Wed. 9–6, Thurs. 9–9.*

Situated on a 26-acre site facing the Chugach Mountains, the extraordinary **Alaska Native Heritage Center** contains a spacious Welcome House that introduces you to Alaska's

Native peoples through displays, artifacts, photographs, demonstrations, performances, and films. You then head outside to explore five village exhibits, which circle a small lake. At each of these you will see traditional structures and Alaska Natives demonstrating their heritage. A café and gift shop are here as well. *8800 Heritage Center Dr. (Glenn Hwy. at Muldoon Rd.), 5 mi east of downtown, tel. 907/330–8000 or 800/315–6608, www.alaskanative.net. Admission: $21 ($30 including round-trip transportation from downtown). Open daily 9–6.*

If you have the time, take a taxi to the **Lake Hood floatplane base,** where colorful aircraft come and go almost constantly in the summer months. The best vantage point is from the patio of the lounge at the **Millennium Anchorage Hotel** (4800 Spenard Rd., tel. 907/243–2300 or 800/544–0553).

Shopping

During the summer, Anchorage's **Saturday Market** (tel. 907/272–5634) fills the parking lot at 3rd Avenue and E Street from 10 to 6; browse here for Alaskan-made crafts, fine arts, ethnic imports, and food.

A number of Anchorage shops sell quality Native Alaskan artwork, and one of the best is **Tundra Arts** (425 D St., tel. 907/276–0190). It's a bit out of the way, but the gift shop inside the **Alaska Native Medical Center** (4315 Diplomacy Dr., off E. Tudor Rd., tel. 907/729–1122) displays an outstanding collection of Native pieces.

Artwork by Alaskan artists, both Native and non-Native, can be found at **Artique Ltd.** (314 G St., tel. 907/277–1663, www.artiqueltd.com). The **Decker/Morris Gallery** (621 W. 6th St., tel. 907/272–1489) has Native and non-Native Alaskan art. For "wearable art" and one-of-a-kind designs in polar fleece apparel, stop in at designer **Tracy Anna Bader's** (416 G St., tel. 907/278–9327) boutique. An option for warm wear is the **Oomingmak Musk Ox Producers Co-op** (corner of 6th Ave. and H St., tel. 907/272–9225 or 888/360–9665, www.qiviut.com), where Native Alaskan villagers hand-knit scarves and hats from the soft-as-cashmere underwool of the musk ox into traditional designs. **Moose Hollow Gifts** (720 D St., tel. 907/274–4215) is the place to go for distinctive Eskimo-style "parkys" (parkas) made by **Laura Wright Alaskan Parkys** (www.alaskan.com/parkys). **Cook Inlet Book Company** (415 W. 5th Ave., tel. 907/258–4544 or 800/240–4148, www.alaskasbooks.com) has a huge selection of Alaskan titles.

Wolf Song (corner of 6th Ave. and C St., tel. 907/274–9653 or 800/243–9653, www.wolfsongalaska.org) is a non-profit gift shop with wildlife art and educational material about wolves.

Frozen seafood and smoked fish are available from **10th and M Seafoods** (1020 M St., tel. 907/272–3474 or 800/770–2722). **New Sagaya's City Market** (900 W. 13th Ave., tel. 907/274–6173 or 800/764–1001) sells an excellent selection of fresh seafood. Both places will also ship seafood for you.

Entertainment

Take a goofy, off-kilter romp across Alaska at the "Whale Fat Follies" Tuesday through Saturday evenings in the **Fly By Night Club** (3300 Spenard Rd., tel. 907/279–7726, www.flybynightclub.com). Mr. Whitekeys is the master of ceremonies for this musical extravaganza of bad taste, accomplished singing, witty skewering of local politicians, and lots of jokes about the Alaskan staples Spam and duct tape. The comedy gets a bit bawdy and may offend some people (which is precisely what Mr. Whitekeys intends).

Outdoor Activities and Sports

BIKING AND HIKING

The Tony Knowles Coastal Trail and other trails in Anchorage are used by cyclists, runners, and walkers. The trail from Westchester Lagoon at the end of 15th Avenue runs 2 mi to Earthquake Park and, beyond that, 9 mi out to Kincaid Park. For bike rentals, contact **Downtown Bicycle Rental** (245 W. 5th Ave., tel. 907/279–5293, www.alaska-bike-rentals.com).

Dining

$$$–$$$$ ✕ **Club Paris.** Alaska's oldest steak house, Club Paris has been here since 1957, and repeat visitors are likely to meet the same waitstaff they saw 20 years ago. The restaurant is filled with dark wood and relics from the 1920s. Meals are equally traditional: tender, flavorful steaks of all kinds,

including a 4-inch-thick filet mignon. If you need to wait for a table, have a martini at the bar and order the hors d'oeuvres platter—a sampler of steak, cheese, and prawns that could be a meal for two people. *417 W. 5th Ave., tel. 907/277–6332. AE, D, DC, MC, V.*

$$$–$$$$ ✗ **Marx Bros. Café.** The fusion cuisine here shows that frontier cooking is much more than a kettle in the kitchen. Among the multicultural specialties of the house is baked halibut with a macadamia crust served with coconut curry and mango chutney. *627 W. 3rd Ave., tel. 907/278–2133. Reservations essential. AE, DC, MC, V. No lunch.*

$$–$$$$ ✗ **Ristorante Orso.** One of Anchorage's culinary stars, Ristorante Orso ("bear" in Italian) evokes the earthiness of a Tuscan villa. Alaskan touches flavor rustic Italian dishes, including traditional pastas, fresh seafood, and wood-grilled meats. Of the locally famous desserts, most notable is a molten chocolate cake served with vanilla ice cream, Sambuca syrup, and coffee-bean brittle. The large bar serves the same menu. *737 W. 5th Ave., tel. 907/222–3232. AE, D, DC, MC, V.*

$$–$$$$ ✗ **Sacks Café.** This bright and colorful restaurant serves American cuisine such as butternut squash ravioli with a shallot saffron sauce; rack of New Zealand lamb; and free-range chicken stuffed with prosciutto, spinach, caramelized onion, and Romano. Be sure to ask about the daily specials. Fresh flowers adorn all tables, and singles congregate in the friendly separate bar area. The café is especially crowded during lunch, served 11–2:30. Sack's Saturday and Sunday brunch menu includes eggs Benedict, a Mexican scrambled egg dish called migas, and various salads and sandwiches. *328 G St., tel. 907/276–3546. Reservations essential. AE, MC, V.*

$$–$$$$ ✗ **Simon & Seafort's Saloon and Grill.** This is the place to enjoy a great view across Cook Inlet while dining on consistently fine Alaskan seafood or rock-salt-roasted prime rib. The bar is a good spot for appetizers, including beer-batter halibut and potatoes Gorgonzola, but you can also order from the full menu. *420 L St., tel. 907/274–3502. AE, DC, MC, V.*

BREWPUBS

Glacier BrewHouse. Wood-fired pizza, fresh seafood, and rotisserie-grilled meats complement the home-brewed beer served here. The stylish space has high ceilings and a central fireplace; the mood is loud and jovial, and you can watch the hardworking chefs in the open kitchen. *737 W. 5th Ave., tel. 907/274–2739. AE, DC, MC, V.*

Humpy's Great Alaskan Alehouse. This immensely popular restaurant and bar has more than 40 draft beers on tap and cranks out huge plates of halibut burgers, health-nut chicken, and smoked-salmon Caesar salad. Humpy's has live music most evenings, so don't expect quiet (or a smoke-free atmosphere) in this hopping singles' spot. *610 W. 6th Ave., tel. 907/276–2337. AE, D, DC, MC, V.*

Snowgoose Restaurant and Sleeping Lady Brewing Company. This brewpub is notable for its large deck overlooking Cook Inlet, Mt. Susitna (the Sleeping Lady), and—on a clear day—Mt. McKinley. The menu includes pizzas, burgers, and pasta, along with seafood specials each evening. *717 W. 3rd Ave., tel. 907/277–7727. AE, MC, V.*

Cordova

Cordova is decidedly off the beaten path, and only a few of the smaller cruise ships visit. If yours does, consider yourself lucky. This is the real thing, a peaceful coastal Alaskan town with no roads to the outside and some marvelous sights.

Perched on Orca Inlet in eastern Prince William Sound, Cordova began life early in the 20th century as the port city for the Copper River–Northwestern Railway, which was built to serve the Kennicott copper mines 191 mi away in the Wrangell Mountains. With the mines and the railroad shut down since 1938, Cordova's economy now depends heavily on fishing. Attempts to develop a road along the abandoned railroad line connecting to the state highway system were dashed by the 1964 earthquake, so Cordova remains isolated. Access to the community is limited to airplane or ferry. A small town with the spectacular backdrop of snowy Mt. Eccles, Cordova is the gateway to the Copper River delta—one of the great birding areas of North America.

Coming Ashore

Cruise ships dock at the boat harbor, and Cordova is just a short walk uphill from here. Ships are met by tour buses from **Copper River & Northwest Tours** (tel. 907/424–5356, www.northernnightsinn.com), or you can catch a cab. **Cordova Taxicab** (tel. 907/424–5151) provides half-hour tours of town for $15 per person.

Pick up maps and tour brochures from the **Cordova Chamber of Commerce Visitor Center** (401 1st St., tel. 907/424–7260, www.cordovachamber.com).

Exploring Cordova

The **Cordova Museum** emphasizes Native artifacts as well as pioneer, mining, and fishing history. Displays include an 1840s handcrafted lighthouse lens and a stuffed 800-pound leatherback turtle. Afternoon video programs and an informative brochure outline a self-guided walking tour of the town's historical buildings. The gift shop sells masks, pottery, and children's and local history books. *622 1st St., tel. 907/424–6665. Admission: $1. Open Mon.–Sat. 10–6, Sun. 2–4.*

The **Million Dollar Bridge,** at Mile 48 on the Copper River Highway, provides a perfect vantage point from which to see the **Childs Glacier.** Although there is no visitor center, a covered viewing area right next to the bridge enables you to watch the face of the glacier and read the informational plaques while you wait for a huge chunk of ice to topple into the river. The waves produced by falling ice frequently wash migrating salmon onto the riverbank, and the local brown bears have been known to patrol the river's edge looking for an easy meal, so keep your eyes wide open.

Guided Tours

Copper River & Northwest Tours (tel. 907/424–5356, www.northernnightsinnc.om) provides bus tours to the Million Dollar Bridge and other sights. **Cordova Air Service** (tel. 907/424–3289, 800/424–7608 in Alaska) leads aerial tours of Prince William Sound on planes with wheels or floats.

Shopping

At **Orca Book & Sound Co.** (507 1st St., tel. 907/424–5305), the walls often double as a gallery for local works or traveling exhibits, and the store specializes in old, rare, out-of-print, and first-edition books, especially Alaskana. In the back is the Killer Whale Café.

Dining

$ ✕ Killer Whale Café. Have a breakfast of espresso and baked goods or an omelet at this bookstore café. For lunch you can choose from a deli menu of soups, salads, and sandwiches, followed by a homemade dessert. On the back balcony, tables overlook the harbor. *507 1st St., tel. 907/424–7733. No credit cards.*

Denali National Park and Preserve

Anchorage serves as a point of departure for trips to spectacular **Denali National Park and Preserve** (tel. 907/683–2294, www.nps.gov/dena), 240 mi to the north. This 6-million-acre national park is a fine place to see wildlife, including bear, caribou, moose, and wolves. Nowhere in the world is there more stunning background scenery to these wildlife riches, with 20,320-foot **Mt. McKinley** looming above forested valleys, tundra-topped hills, and the glacier-covered peaks of the Alaska Range. Also commonly known by its Athabascan Indian name, **Denali**—"The High One"—North America's highest mountain is the world's tallest when measured from base to top: the great mountain rises more than 18,000 ft above surrounding lowlands. Unfortunately for visitors with little time to spend in the area, McKinley is wreathed in clouds on average two days of every three in the summer.

Vegetation in Denali consists largely of coniferous forest (taiga) and open tundra, with permanent snow and ice at the higher elevations. Nearly every kind of wild creature that walks or flies in South Central and Interior Alaska inhabits the park. Thirty-eight species of mammals reside here, from wolves and bears to little brown bats and pygmy shrews that weigh a fraction of an ounce. While traveling the only road into the park you can expect to see Dall sheep finding their way across high meadows, grizzlies and caribou lingering at stream bottoms, moose traversing forested areas, and the occasional wolf or fox darting across the road.

Exploring Denali National Park and Preserve

You can take a tour bus or the Alaska Railroad from Anchorage to the Denali National Park entrance. Both Princess and Holland America attach their own rail cars behind these trains for a more luxurious experience. Most cruise passengers stay one or two nights in hotels at a riverside settlement called Denali Park, just outside the park entrance. Shuttle buses provide transportation from your hotel to the park's busy **Visitor Access Center,** where you can watch slide shows on the park, purchase maps and books, or check the schedule for naturalist presentations and sled-dog demonstrations. Access to the park itself is by bus on day tours. If you are not visiting Denali as part of your cruise package, call 907/276–7234 or 800/276–7234 to make reservations for a bus tour ($41–$76 per person, including a snack or box lunch). Park entrance is $5, or free for senior citizens with a Golden Age Passport.

The 90-mi **Denali Park Road** winds from the park entrance to Wonder Lake and Kantishna, the historic mining community in the heart of the park. Public access along this road is limited to tour and shuttle buses that depart from the Visitor Access Center. The Park Road is paved for the first 14 mi and gravel the rest of the way. Bus drivers are not in a hurry (the speed limit is 35 mph) and make frequent stops to view wildlife or to explain Denali's natural history.

Your narrated park tour will probably last around six hours round-trip and will take you as far as **Polychrome Pass,** 53 mi each way. Longer trips to **Eielson Visitor Center** (eight hours round-trip) or **Wonder Lake** (11 hours round-trip) provide a better chance to see Mt. McKinley and more of the park but may not be available unless you spend an additional night in the Denali area. Check with your cruise to see if these more expensive options are available. The Eielson–to–Wonder Lake stretch is particularly beautiful from mid-August to early September, when the tundra is ablaze with autumn's yellows, reds, and oranges.

Outdoor Activities and Sports

HIKING

Day hiking can be supreme in Denali. A system of forest and tundra trails starts at the park entrance. These range from easy to challenging and are suitable for visitors of all ages and hiking abilities. Get hiking information and trail maps—along with bear and moose safety tips—from the Visitor Access Center. Rangers lead hikes daily in summer.

RAFTING

Several rafting companies operate along the Parks Highway near the entrance to Denali and offer daily trips in the fairly placid stretches of the Nenana River and through the white water of Nenana River canyon. Gear and a courtesy pickup from your hotel are included. **Alaska Raft Adventures** books white-water and scenic raft trips along Nenana River through Denali Park Resorts (tel. 907/276–7234 or 800/276–7234, fax 907/258–3668, www.denaliparkresorts.com). **Denali Outdoor Center** (tel. 907/683–1925 or 888/303–1925, www.denalioutdoorcenter.com) takes adventuresome people on guided trips down the Nenana River rapids in inflatable rafts and kayaks. **Denali Raft Adventures** (tel. 907/683–2234 or 888/683–2234, www.denaliraft.com) launches its rafts several times daily on a variety of scenic and white-water Nenana River raft trips. **Nenana Raft Adventures** (tel. 907/683–7238 or 800/789–7238, www.raftdenali.com) runs four- and six-hour rafting trips along Nenana River.

Dining

$–$$$ ✕ **Lynx Creek Pizza.** Located in a cluster of hotels and tourist places just outside the park entrance, this casual restaurant is a popular hangout, good for pizza, sandwiches, salads, ice cream, and beer on tap. Order at the front and grab a seat at picnic-table benches. *Mile 238.6 Parks Hwy., tel. 907/683–2547. AE, D, DC, MC, V.*

$–$$ ✕ **McKinley/Denali Salmon Bake.** Looking as though it might blow away in a stiff wind, this rustic hillside eatery serves breakfast, lunch, and dinner. Baked fresh salmon tops the menu; steaks, burgers, and chicken are also available. Shuttle service is provided to area hotels. *Mile 238.5 Parks Hwy., tel. 907/683–2733. AE, D, DC, MC, V.*

Glacier Bay National Park and Preserve

Cruising Glacier Bay is like revisiting the Little Ice Age, when glaciers covered much of the northern hemisphere. This is one of the few places in the world where you can get within ¼ mi of tidewater glaciers, which have their base at the water's edge. Six of them line the 60 mi of narrow fjords at the northern end of the Inside Passage. Huge chunks of ice break off the glaciers and crash into the water, producing a dazzling show known as calving.

Although the Tlingit have lived in the area for 10,000 years, the bay was first popularized by naturalist John Muir, who visited in 1879. Just 100 years before, the bay had been completely choked with ice. By 1916, though, the ice had retreated 65 mi—the most rapid glacial retreat ever recorded. To preserve its clues to the world's geological history, Glacier Bay was declared a national monument in 1925. It became a national park in 1980. Today several of the glaciers in the west arm are advancing again, but very slowly.

Competition for entry permits into Glacier Bay is fierce among cruise ships. To protect the humpback whale, which feeds here in summer, the Park Service limits the number of ships that can call. Check your cruise brochure to make sure that Glacier Bay is included in your sailing. Most ships that do visit spend at least one full day exploring the park. There are no shore excursions or landings in the bay, but a Park Service naturalist boards every cruise ship to provide narration on its history and scientific importance. It is often misty or rainy, so rain gear is essential. The average summer temperature is 50°F. As always in Alaska, be prepared for the cold. Also, be sure to bring binoculars, extra film, and, if you have one, a telephoto lens.

The glaciers that most cruise passengers see are in the west arm of Glacier Bay. Ships linger in front of five glaciers so you can admire their stunning faces. First, most ships stop briefly at **Reid Glacier** before continuing on to **Lamplugh Glacier**—one of the bluest in the park—at the mouth of Johns Hopkins Inlet. Next is massive **Johns Hopkins Glacier** at the end of the inlet, where you're likely to see a continuous shower of calving ice. Sometimes there are so many icebergs in the inlet that ships must avoid the area. Moving farther north, to the end of the western arm, **Margerie Glacier** is also quite active. Adjacent is **Grand Pacific Glacier,** the largest glacier in the park.

Your experience in Glacier Bay will depend partly on the size of your ship. Ocean liners tend to stay midchannel, while small yachtlike ships spend more time closer to shore. On a smaller ship you may get a better view of the calving ice and wildlife—such as brown and black bears, mountain

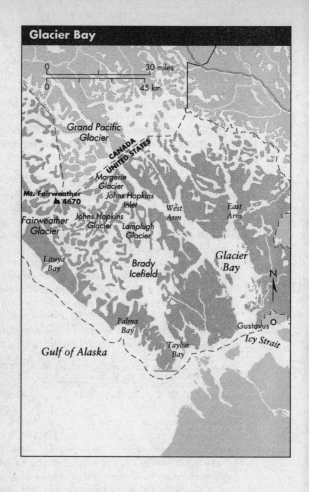

Glacier Bay

0   30 miles

0   45 km.

Grand Pacific Glacier

CANADA
UNITED STATES

Margerie Glacier

Mt. Fairweather ▲ 4670

Johns Hopkins Inlet

West Arm

East Arm

Fairweather Glacier

Johns Hopkins Glacier

Lamplugh Glacier

Lituya Bay

Brady Icefield

Glacier Bay

N

Palma Bay

Gustavus

Icy Strait

Gulf of Alaska

Taylor Bay

goats, moose, and seals with their pups—but on a big-
ship, you'll get a loftier perspective. Both types of vessels
come within ¼ mi of the glaciers themselves.

Haines

Unlike most other cities in Southeast Alaska, Haines can
be reached by road; the 152-mi (245-km) Haines Highway
connects with the Alaska Highway at Haines Junction. In
1879, two white men paddled a canoe into the area—the
missionary S. Hall Young and famed naturalist John Muir.
Young was intent upon establishing a Presbyterian mission,
and with the blessing of local Tlingit chiefs, they chose the
site that later became Haines. They could hardly have
picked a more beautiful spot. The town sits on a heavily
wooded peninsula with magnificent views of Portage Cove
and the Coastal Mountain Range. Juneau is 80 mi to the
south by way of fjordlike Lynn Canal.

The town has two distinct personalities. On the north side
of the Haines Highway is the section of Haines that de-
veloped around the Presbyterian mission. After its missionary beginnings, the town served as the trailhead for the
Jack Dalton Trail into the Yukon during the 1897 gold rush
to the Klondike. The following year, when gold was discovered on the nearby Porcupine River, Haines became a
supply center and base for those goldfields as well. Today
things are quieter; the town's streets are orderly, its homes
are well kept, and for the most part it looks a great deal
like any other Alaska seacoast community.

South of the highway, the town looks like a military post,
which is exactly what it was for nearly half a century. In
1903 the U.S. Army established Fort William Henry Seward
at Portage Cove just south of town. The post (renamed
Chilkoot Barracks in 1922) was the only military base in
the territory until World War II. In 1939, the army built
the Alaska Highway and the Haines Highway to connect
Alaska with the other states.

After the war the post closed down, and a group of veter-
ans purchased the property from the government. They
changed its name to Port Chilkoot and created residences,

businesses, and an Alaska Native arts center from the officers' houses and military buildings that surrounded the old fort's parade ground. Eventually Port Chilkoot merged with the city of Haines. Although the two areas are now officially one municipality, the old military post with its grassy parade ground is still referred to as Ft. Seward.

Today the community of Haines is recognized for the Native American dance and culture center at Ft. Seward as well as for the superb fishing, camping, and outdoor recreation at Chilkoot Lake, Portage Cove, Mosquito Lake, and Chilkat State Park on the shores of Chilkat Inlet, from which you can see the Davidson and Rainbow glaciers across the water.

Haines has not been a major stop for large cruise ships, but that may be changing as the community warms to tourism.

Coming Ashore

Cruise ships and catamaran ferries dock in front of Ft. Seward, and downtown Haines is just a short walk away (about ½ mi). You can pick up walking-tour maps of Haines at the **visitor center** (tel. 907/766–2234 or 800/458–3579, www.haines.ak.us) on 2nd Avenue. Most cruise lines provide complimentary shuttle service to downtown. Taxis are always standing by; hour-long taxi tours of the town cost $10 per person. A one-way trip between the pier and town costs $5. For a pickup, call **Haines Taxi and Tours** (tel. 907/766–3138) or the **New Other Guys Taxi** (tel. 907/766–3257).

Two local operators provide day trips from nearby Skagway if your ship doesn't stop in Haines. Transportation is by high-speed catamaran ferries, which depart several times a day. **Alaska Fjordlines** (tel. 907/766–3395 or 800/320–0146, www.alaskafjordlines.com) operates a high-speed catamaran between Haines and Juneau, stopping along the way to watch sea lions and other marine mammals. **Chilkat Cruises** (tel. 907/766–2100 or 888/766–2103, www.chilkatcruises.com) provides a passenger catamaran ferry between Skagway and Haines, with service several times a day in the summer.

Exploring Haines

Numbers in the margin correspond to points of interest on the Haines map.

① The **Sheldon Museum and Cultural Center,** near the foot of Main Street, houses Native artifacts—including famed Chilkat blankets—plus gold-rush memorabilia such as Jack Dalton's sawed-off shotgun. *11 Main St., tel. 907/766–2366, www.sheldonmuseum.org. Admission: $3. Open mid-May–mid-Sept., weekdays 11–6, weekends 2–6, and whenever cruise ships are in port; mid-Sept.–mid-May, weekdays 1–4.*

② The Chilkat Indian Dancers perform at the **Tribal House** on the Ft. Seward parade grounds. This unique theatrical production includes elaborate carved masks and impressive costumes as dancers tell ancient Tlingit legends. Performances are several times a week and when cruise ships are in port. *Ft. Seward, tel. 907/766–2540, www.tresham.com/show. Admission: $10.*

③ At **Alaska Indian Arts,** a nonprofit organization dedicated to the revival of Tlingit art forms, you'll see Native carvers making totems, metalsmiths working silver, and weavers making blankets. *Ft. Seward parade ground, tel. 907/766–2160, www.alaskaindianarts.com. Open weekdays 8–5 and whenever cruise ships are in port.*

Celebrating Haines's location in the "Valley of the Eagles" **④** is the **American Bald Eagle Foundation.** Inside this small museum is a diorama with stuffed local animals, but the primary focus here is bald eagles. You'll learn about these majestic birds and the nearby Chilkat Bald Eagle Preserve through lectures, displays, and videos. *2nd Ave. and Haines Hwy., tel. 907/766–3094, www.baldeagles.org. Admission: $3. Open May–Nov., daily 8–6 and whenever cruise ships are in port.*

Outdoor Activities and Sports

HIKING

Battery Point Trail is a fairly level path that hugs the shoreline for 2½ mi, providing fine views across Lynn Canal. The trail begins at Portage Cove Campground (1 mi east of Haines). For other hikes, pick up a copy of "Haines Is for

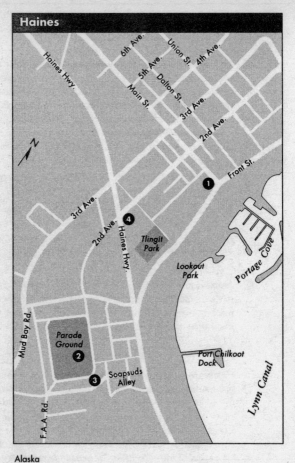

Haines

Hikers" at the **visitor center** (112 2nd Ave., tel. 907/766–
2234 or 800/458–3579, www.haines.ak.us).

Dining

$$–$$$ ✕ **The Wild Strawberry.** Just a few doors down from the
visitor center, this chic café offers a bright escape from a
rainy day. Owned by a family of commercial fishermen, the
kitchen serves just-caught salmon, halibut, and crab. The
outside deck is a delight on sunny afternoons. *138 2nd Ave.,
tel. 907/766–3608. MC, V.*

$–$$$ ✕ **Bamboo Room.** Pop culture meets greasy spoon in this
unassuming coffee shop with red vinyl booths. The menu
includes sandwiches, burgers, fried chicken, chili, and hal-
ibut fish-and-chips, but the place really is at its best for an
all-American breakfast (available till 3 PM). *2nd Ave. near
Main St., tel. 907/766–2800, fax 907/766–3374, AE, D,
DC, MC, V.*

$–$$$ ✕ **Commander's Room Restaurant.** Facing Ft. Seward's
parade ground, this restaurant inside the Hotel Halsingland
is a good stop for tasty fish-and-chips and burgers. The Halsingland prepares a delicious all-you-can-eat lunchtime
salmon bake ($25) at the Tlingit tribal house when cruise
ships are in port. *Ft. Seward, tel. 907/766–2000 or 800/
542–6363. AE, DC, MC, V.*

Saloons

Commercial fisherfolk gather nightly at the circa 1907
Harbor Bar (Front St. at the Harbor, tel. 907/766–2444)
next to the Lighthouse Restaurant. Sometimes there's live
music. It's colorful but can get a little loud at night.

Homer

Of the hundreds of thousands of cruise passengers who visit
Alaska each year, only a very few get to see Homer. It's a
shame. In a state of beautiful places, Homer's scenic setting on Kachemak Bay, surrounded by mountains, spruce
forest, and glaciers makes it an ideal destination. The town
is famous for its halibut and salmon fishing and serves as
a base for bear-viewing flights. In addition, Homer is one
of the top arts communities in Alaska, with several first-
rate galleries, a theater company, and an active music and
dance scene.

Homer lies at the base of a 4-mi-long (6-km-long) sandy spit that juts into Kachemak Bay. The town was founded just before the turn of the 20th century as a gold-prospecting camp and later became a coal-mining headquarters. Today Homer is a funky fishing port with art galleries and beautiful bay views. It's a favorite weekend spot for Anchorage residents needing a change of scene and weather.

Coming Ashore

Large cruise ships do not stop in Homer, but the town is visited by smaller ships, along with Alaska Marine Highway ferries. In addition, Homer is easily reached by car from the town of Seward, where Gulf of Alaska cruises often start or finish. It's a five-hour drive by car from Anchorage. Scheduled air service is available from Anchorage several times a day on **Era Aviation** (tel. 907/266–8394 or 800/866–8394, www.eraaviation.com). To get here by bus from Anchorage or Seward, contact **Homer Stage Line** (tel. 907/235–2252).

State ferries dock at the end of the Homer Spit. Fishing charters, restaurants, and shops line the Spit, or you can take a taxi to town, where local galleries and additional dining are found. For door-to-door service, call **Chuck's Cab** (tel. 907/235–2489). A ride from the Spit into town will cost you $10 one-way. You can also ride the **Homer Trolley** (tel. 907/235–8624), which runs every hour from 10 AM to 6 PM between the Spit and downtown. The fare is $5.

Exploring Homer

For an outstanding introduction to Homer's history—both human and natural—visit the **Pratt Museum,** where you can see a saltwater aquarium and exhibits on pioneers, flora and fauna, Native Alaskans, and the 1989 *Exxon Valdez* oil spill. You can spy on wildlife with robotic video cameras set up on a seabird rookery and a bear viewing area. Outside is a wildflower garden and a short nature trail. The museum also leads 1½-hour walking tours of the harbor for $5 per person several times a week. *Bartlett St., off Pioneer Ave., tel. 907/235–8635, www.prattmuseum.org. Admission: $6. Open daily 10–6.*

The **Islands and Oceans Visitor Center** houses fascinating interactive exhibits detailing the Alaska Maritime Na-

tional Wildlife Refuge, which encompasses some 2,500 islands along the coast of Alaska. A path leads along Beluga Slough to Bishops Beach, a favorite place for a low-tide
beach walk. *95 Sterling Hwy., tel. 907/235–6961, www.
islandsandocean.org. Admission: Free. Open late May–early
Sept., daily 9–6; early Sept.–late May, Mon.–Sat. 9–5.*

Kachemak Bay abounds in wildlife. Shore excursions or local
tour operators take you to bird rookeries in the bay or to
gravel beaches for clam digging. Most charter-fishing trips
include an opportunity to view whales, seals, sea otters, por-
poises, and seabirds close-up. Walking along the docks on
Homer Spit at the end of the day you can watch commercial fishing boats and charter boats unload their catch.
The bay supports a large population of bald eagles, gulls,
murres, puffins, and other birds.

Directly across Kachemak Bay from the end of the Homer
Spit, **Halibut Cove** is a small community of people who make
their living on the bay or by selling handicrafts. **Central Charter Booking Agency** (tel. 907/235–7847 or 800/478–7847,
www.centralcharter.com) runs frequent boats to the cove
from Homer. Halibut Cove has several art galleries and a
restaurant that serves local seafood. The cove itself is lovely,
especially during salmon runs, when fish leap and splash
in the clear water.

Seldovia, isolated across the bay from Homer, retains the
charm of an earlier Alaska. The town's Russian heritage is
evident in its onion-dome church and its name, derived
from a Russian place-name meaning "herring bay." Those
who fish use plenty of herring for bait, catching salmon, halibut, and king or Dungeness crab. You'll find excellent fishing whether you drop your line into the deep waters of
Kachemak Bay or cast into the surf for silver salmon on the
shore of Outside Beach, near town. Self-guided hiking and
berry picking in late July are other options. Seldovia can be
reached from Homer by tour boat; contact **Central Charter
Booking Agency** (tel. 907/235–7847 or 800/478–7847,
www.centralcharter.com). The dock of the small-boat harbor is in the center of town—allowing for easy exploration.
Rent a mountain bike from the **Buzz** (tel. 907/234–7479).
Kayak'Atak (tel. 907/234–7425, www.alaska.net/~kayaks)
guides sea-kayak trips in the area.

Shopping

The galleries in downtown Homer and on the Spit often highlight works by local residents. Head to **Bunnell Street Gallery** (corner of Main and Bunnell Sts., tel. 907/235–2662) for a diverse and surprisingly creative selection of pieces. **Ptarmigan Arts** (471 E. Pioneer Ave., tel. 907/235–5345) is packed with works from local artists, most of whom work at this pseudo-cooperative gallery.

Alaska Wild Berry Products (528 E. Pioneer Ave., tel. 907/235–8858 or 800/280–2927) manufactures jams, jellies, sauces, syrups, and chocolate-covered candies made from wild berries handpicked on the Kenai Peninsula. Also here is a large selection of Alaska-theme gifts, souvenirs, trinkets, and clothing; shipping is available.

Dining

$$–$$$ ✕ **Café Cups.** It's hard to miss this place as you head down Pioneer Avenue—look for the huge namesake cups on the building's facade. A longtime Homer favorite, Cups serves lunches and dinners that make the most of the local seafood, complemented by a terrific wine list. It's one of the few small restaurants in Alaska where the menu includes vegetarian dishes. The outside deck is a fine place to enjoy a lazy morning while savoring your eggs Florentine. *162 W. Pioneer Ave., tel. 907/235–8330. MC, V.*

$$–$$$ ✕ **Saltry in Halibut Cove.** This restaurant serves local seafood as sushi or prepares it with curries and pastas. Salads from local gardens and freshly baked bread round out the meal. Wash it all down with your choice from a wide assortment of imported beers. The deck overlooks the boat dock and the cove. *Take the Danny J ferry ($22 round-trip) from Homer harbor, Halibut Cove, tel. 907/235–7847 or 800/478–7847 Central Charters. Reservations essential. D, MC, V. Closed Labor Day–Memorial Day.*

$–$$ ✕ **Two Sisters.** For a delightful taste of the real Homer, visit this inviting eatery, just a block from Bishops Beach and the Ocean and Islands Visitor Center. Two Sisters fills with a mixed crowd of fishermen, writers, and local businesspeople drinking espresso, talking politics, and sampling pastries to die for. Focaccia sandwiches, savory danishes, and deep-dish pizza are all on the menu. The wraparound deck has tables for warm summer afternoons. *233 E. Bunnell*

St., tel. 907/235–2280, www.twosistersbakery.net. No credit cards.

Saloons

The **Salty Dawg Saloon** (tel. 907/235–9990) is famous all over Alaska. Fishermen, sailors, and carpenters have been holding court for decades in this friendly and noisy pub with sawdust floors and walls caked with all sorts of flotsam. Today they're joined by college kids working in the gift shops, retirees, and tourists. Near the end of the Spit, the Salty Dawg is easy to find; just look for the "lighthouse."

Juneau

Juneau owes its origins to a trio of colorful characters: two pioneers, Joe Juneau and Dick Harris, and a Tlingit chief named Kowee, who discovered rich reserves of gold in the stream that now runs through the middle of town. That was in 1880, and shortly after the discovery a modest stampede led first to the establishment of a camp, then a town, then the Alaska territorial (now state) capital.

For nearly 60 years after Juneau's founding, gold remained the mainstay of the economy. In its heyday, the Alaska Juneau gold mine was the biggest low-grade-ore mine in the world. Then, during World War II, the government decided it needed Juneau's manpower for the war effort, and the mines ceased operations. After the war, mining failed to start up again, and the government became the city's principal employer. Today tourism is equally important to the local economy. On summer days several cruise ships anchor along the downtown docks, sending thousands of travelers off to explore this small city, ride the tram up Mt. Roberts, watch bears from a floatplane, land on a glacier in a helicopter, or paddle away in a sea kayak.

Juneau is a charming, cosmopolitan frontier town. It's easy to navigate, has one of the best museums in Alaska, is surrounded by beautiful (and accessible) wilderness, and has a glacier in its backyard. To capture the true frontier ambience, stop by the Red Dog Saloon or the Alaskan Hotel. Both are on the main shopping drag, just a quick walk from the cruise-ship pier.

Coming Ashore

Cruise ships dock or tender passengers ashore on the south edge of town between **Marine Park** and the **Cruise Ship Terminal** near the Mt. Roberts Tram. Several ships can tie up at once, and others anchor a short distance away in the protected harbor. Juneau's downtown shops are a pleasant walk (¼ mi) from the dock. There is also a shuttle bus ($1 round-trip) that runs from the dock to town whenever ships are in town.

Pick up maps, bus schedules, charter-fishing information, and tour brochures at the small kiosks on the pier at Marine Park and in the Cruise Ship Terminal on South Franklin Street. Both are staffed when ships are in port.

You won't need to hire a taxi in downtown Juneau, but several sights—including Mendenhall Glacier, Glacier Gardens, and the Gastineau Salmon Hatchery—are too far to walk to. You can catch a tour bus or a taxi from Marine Park. Another option is the city bus that stops on South Franklin Street. For $1.25, it'll take you within 1 mi of the Mendenhall Visitor Center. **Mendenhall Glacier Tours** (tel. 907/789–5460, www.mightygreattrips.com) provides direct bus transport between downtown and the glacier for $10 round-trip or tours that include time at the glacier for $20 per person.

Exploring Juneau

Numbers in the margin correspond to points of interest on the Juneau map.

❶ Cruise ships dock along busy **South Franklin Street** near the Mt. Roberts Tram. A number of the buildings here and on Front Street, which intersects South Franklin several blocks north, are among the oldest and most interesting in the city. The small **Alaskan Hotel** (167 S. Franklin St., tel. 907/586–1000 or 800/327–9347) was called "a pocket edition of the best hotels on the Pacific Coast" when it opened in 1913. The building, which has been lovingly restored with period trappings, operates as an active hotel. The barroom's massive, mirrored oak bar, accented by Tiffany lamps and panels, is a particular delight. The **Alaska Steam Laundry Building** (174 S. Franklin St.,), a 1901 structure with a windowed turret, now houses a great collection of photos from

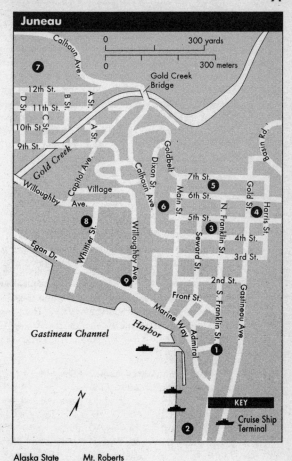

Juneau

Calhoun Ave.

Gold Creek Bridge

12th St.
11th St.
10th St.
9th St.

D St.
B St.
A St.
C St.
A St.

Gold Creek

Willoughby

Basin Rd.

Goldbelt
7th St.
6th St.
5th St.
4th St.
3rd St.
2nd St.

Dixon St.
Main St.
N. Franklin St.
Gold St.
Harris St.
Seward St.
S. Franklin St.
Gastineau Ave.

Capitol Ave.
Calhoun Ave.
Village Ave.
Whittier St.
Willoughby Ave.
Egan Dr.

Front St.
Marine Way
Admiral

Gastineau Channel

Harbor

KEY

Cruise Ship Terminal

0   300 yards
0   300 meters

N

Juneau's past, a popular espresso shop (Heritage Coffee Co. tel. 907/586–1752), and several stores.

❷ For a great view of the harbor, take the **Mt. Roberts Tram** to an observation deck 2,000 ft above Juneau. Walking paths radiate from the mountaintop visitor center, which also houses retail shops, a restaurant and bar, a nature center, and an auditorium that shows a film on Tlingit Native culture. You can catch the tram from the base terminal downtown. The tram and all facilities are wheelchair accessible. *490 S. Franklin St., tel. 907/463–3412 or 888/461–8726, www.alaska.net/~junotram. Admission: Unlimited single-day rides $21.95. Open daily 9–9.*

❸ At the corner of Seward and 4th Streets is the **Alaska State Capitol,** constructed in 1930, with pillars of southeastern Alaska marble. The structure now houses the governor's office, and the state legislature meets here from January through May each year. Pick up a self-guided tour pamphlet as you enter. *tel. 907/465–2479. Open weekdays 8–5.*

❹ At the top of the hill on 5th Street is little **St. Nicholas Russian Orthodox Church,** built in 1894, and the oldest Russian church building in Southeast Alaska. Here you can see icons that date from the 1700s. *326 5th St., off Gold St., tel. 907/780–6320. Admission: $2. Tours mid-May–Sept., Mon.–Sat. noon–6.*

❺ The **Wickersham State Historical Site,** the 1899 residence of James Wickersham, a pioneer judge and delegate to Congress, houses memorabilia from the judge's travels, ranging from rare Native American basketry and ivory carvings to historic photos, 47 diaries, and a Chickering grand piano that came "round the horn" to Alaska when the Russians still ruled the region. The tour provides a glimpse into the life of this dynamic man and also includes tea and sourdough cookies. *213 7th St., tel. 907/586–9001, www.dnr.state.ak.us/parks. Admission: Admission and tour $2. Open Thurs.–Tues. 10–noon and 1–5.*

❻ Two fine totem poles flank the entrance to the **Juneau-Douglas City Museum.** Inside, the city's history is relayed through memorabilia, gold-mining exhibits, and videos. *114 W. 4th St., at Main St., tel. 907/586–3572, www.juneau.org/*

parksrec/museum. Admission: $3. Open weekdays 9–5,
weekends 10–5.

❼ **Evergreen Cemetery** is where many Juneau pioneers (including Joe Juneau and Dick Harris) are buried. A mean-
dering gravel path leads through the graveyard, and at the
end of it is the monument commemorating the cremation
spot of Chief Kowee.

❽ The **Alaska State Museum** is one of Alaska's best, with exhibits on the state's history, Native cultures, wildlife, industry, and art. *395 Whittier St., tel. 907/465–2901,*
www.museums.state.ak.us. Admission: $5. Open daily
8:30–5:30.

❾ The **Centennial Hall Visitor Center** has details on local
attractions and nature trails, plus videos for rainy days.
101 Egan Dr., tel. 907/586–2201 or 888/581–2201, www.
traveljuneau.com. Open May–Sept., weekdays 8:30–5,
weekends 9–5; Oct.–Apr., weekdays 9–4.

One of Juneau's most popular sights, **Mendenhall Glacier**
is just 13 mi from downtown. The visitor center has educational exhibits, videos, and natural history walks. Nearby
hiking trails offer magnificent views of the glacier itself. A
visit to the glacier is included in most Juneau bus tours. *tel.*
907/789–0097, www.fs.fed.us/r10/tongass. Admission: $3.
Open daily 8–6:30.

Located 3 mi north of downtown, **Macaulay Salmon Hatchery** is a fine place to learn about salmon and commercial
fishing. An underwater window lets you watch as salmon
fight their way up a fish ladder, and the gift shop sells
salmon products. *2697 Channel Dr., tel. 907/463–4810 or*
877/463–2486, www.dipac.net. Admission: Admission
and tour $3. Open weekdays 10–6, weekends 10–5.

Spread over 50 acres of rain forest 8 mi north of Juneau,
Glacier Gardens Rainforest Adventure contains ponds, waterfalls, hiking paths, and gardens. The roots of fallen trees,
turned upside down and buried in the ground, act as bowls
to hold planters that overflow with begonias, fuchsias, and
petunias. Guided tours (on covered golf carts) carry you
along the 4 mi of paved paths to a dramatic mountainside
overlook. *7600 Glacier Hwy., tel. 907/790–3377, www.*

glaciergardens.com. Admission: $15 including guided tour. Open daily 9–6.

When you're visiting the bars and watering holes of Southeast Alaska, ask for Alaskan Amber, Frontier Beer, or Pale Ale. All are brewed and bottled in Juneau at the **Alaskan Brewing Company,** where you can take a tour and sample the award-winning beers. *5429 Shaune Dr., tel. 907/780–5866, www.alaskanbeer.com. Open Mon.–Sat. 11–5; tours every ½ hr.*

Shopping

South Franklin Street is the place to shop in Juneau. The variety of merchandise is good, though some shops offer an abundance of Made-in-China Alaskan keepsakes. You'll pay high prices for authentic Native handicrafts or hand-knit sweaters.

Annie Kaill's Fine Art and Craft Gallery (244 Front St., tel. 907/586–2880) displays a whimsical mix of original prints, trinkets, jewelry, and ceramics from Alaskan artists. The **Raven's Journey** (439 S. Franklin St., tel. 907/463–4686), across from the tram, specializes in high-quality Alaskan Native masks, grass baskets, carvings, dolls, and ivory pieces.

The **Russian Shop** (389 S. Franklin St., tel. 907/586–2778) houses a repository of icons, samovars, lacquered boxes, nesting dolls, and other items that reflect Alaska's 18th- and 19th-century Russian heritage.

Prints from one of Alaska's best-known artists, Rie Muñoz, are sold at **Decker Gallery** (233 S. Franklin St., tel. 907/463–5536 or 800/463–5536). Her works use stylized designs and bright swirls of colors and often feature Native Alaskans. A fun place to browse is the **Wm. Spear Designs Gallery** (174 S. Franklin St., tel. 907/586–2209) above Heritage Coffee. Spear's colorful enameled pins are witty, creative, amusing, and sometimes simply perverse.

At **Taku Smokeries** (550 S. Franklin St., tel. 907/463–5033 or 800/582–5122), on the south end of town near the cruise-ship docks, you can view the smoking process through large windows and then purchase packaged fish in the deli-style gift shop. It can also ship fish home for you.

Outdoor Activities and Sports

HIKING

Surrounded by the **Tongass National Forest,** America's largest forest, Juneau is a hiker's paradise. The office is 10 mi north of town near the airport; to request trail maps and information, call 907/586–8790, or stop by the Centennial Hall Visitor Center. The Juneau-Douglas City Museum sells a useful booklet: "90 Short Walks Around Juneau" ($7). Good trails begin just behind the Mendenhall Glacier Visitor Center.

Gastineau Guiding (tel. 907/586–2666, www.stepintoalaska. com) leads guided hikes in the Juneau area. A two-hour tour starts at the dock and includes a city tour, a Mt. Roberts tram ride, and a one-hour alpine hike for $48. It also offers a three-hour rain-forest nature tour and walk on Douglas Island for $64.

The **Juneau Parks and Recreation Department** (tel. 907/ 586–5226, 907/586–0428 24-hr info, www.juneau.lib.ak. us/parksrec) sponsors Wednesday-morning and Saturday group hikes on some of the 90 trails around Juneau.

KAYAKING

Auk Ta Shaa Discovery (tel. 907/586–8687 or 800/820–2628, www.goldbelttours.com) leads raft and kayak trips down the Mendenhall River, plus all-day sea-kayaking adventures ($95 per person). Lunch and rain gear are included. Trips leave around 9:30 AM and return about 4 PM, so participation is practical only if your ship makes day-long calls.

Dining

$$–$$$$ ✕ **Dragon Inn.** Chef-owner Peter Lan skillfully blends Alaskan seafood with Asian sauces and cooking techniques in this stylish downtown restaurant. House specialties include Singapore rice noodles with shredded pork, crispy boneless duck, and a pan-fried king salmon fillet served over Chinese vegetables with a light black bean sauce. *213 Front St., tel. 907/586–4888. MC, V. Closed Sun. No lunch Sat.*

$$–$$$$ ✕ **Fiddlehead Restaurant and Bakery.** A favorite with Juneauites, the Fiddlehead is decorated with light wood, stained glass, and modern art and serves generous portions of hearty Alaskan fare. Entrées range from Sicilian fisher-

man's stew to Black Angus meat loaf. Meals are enhanced with homemade bread and desserts from the restaurant's bakery. *429 W. Willoughby Ave., tel. 907/586–3150. AE, D, DC, MC, V.*

$–$$$ ✕ **Hangar on the Wharf.** Come to this Juneau hot spot to gaze at the expansive views of Gastineau Channel and Douglas Island while dining on locally caught halibut or salmon, jambalaya, filet mignon, or great burgers. The Hangar has one of the largest selections of draft beers in Southeast Alaska, with two dozen brews available. *2 Marine Way, tel. 907/586–5018. AE, D, MC, V.*

Saloons

Juneau is one of the best saloon towns in all of Alaska. Try stopping in one of the following:

The Victorian-style **Alaskan Hotel Bar** (167 S. Franklin St., tel. 907/586–1000) is about as funky a place as you'll find in Juneau, with flocked-velvet walls, antique chandeliers above the bar, and vintage Alaskan-frontier brothel decor. Sit back and enjoy the live music or take turns with the locals at the open mike.

The comfortable **Bubble Room** (127 N. Franklin St., tel. 907/586–2660) lounge off the lobby in the Baranof Hotel is quiet and sees (so it is said) more legislative lobbying and decision making than the nearby state capitol building. The music from the piano bar is soft.

The **Red Dog Saloon** (278 S. Franklin St., tel. 907/463–9954), Alaska's best-known saloon, has sawdust on the floors, a mounted bear as well as game trophies on the walls, and lots of historic photos. Every conceivable surface in this two-story bar is cluttered with life preservers, business cards, and college banners. There's live music and the crowd is raucous, especially when cruise ships are in port.

Kenai Peninsula

Salmon and halibut fishing, scenery, and wildlife are the draws of the Kenai Peninsula, which thrusts into the Gulf of Alaska south of Anchorage. Commercial fishing is important to the area's economy, and the city of Kenai, on the peninsula's northwest coast, is the base for the Cook Inlet offshore oil and gas fields.

The area is dotted with roadside campgrounds, and you can explore three major federal holdings on the peninsula—the western end of the sprawling **Chugach National Forest,** the **Kenai National Wildlife Refuge,** and **Kenai Fjords National Park. Portage Glacier,** 50 mi southeast of Anchorage, is a popular stop between Seward and Anchorage. A 6-mi (10-km) side road off the Seward Highway leads to the **Begich-Boggs visitor center** (tel. 907/783–2326) on the shore of Portage Lake. The center houses impressive displays on glaciers, and nearby is a dock that faces the glacier. Unfortunately, the glacier is rapidly receding and is no longer pushing many icebergs into the lake, so the views are not what they once were.

The mountains surrounding Portage Glacier are covered with smaller glaciers. A short hike to Byron Glacier Overlook, about 1 mi west, is popular in the spring and summer. Twice weekly in summer, naturalists lead free treks in search of microscopic ice worms. Keep an eye out for black bears in all the Portage side valleys in the summer.

Ketchikan

At the base of 3,000-foot Deer Mountain, Ketchikan is the definitive Southeast Alaska town. Houses cling to the steep hillsides and the harbors are filled with fishing boats. Until miners and fishermen settled here in the 1880s, the mouth of Ketchikan Creek was a summer fishing camp for the Tlingit people. Today the town runs on fishing, tourism, government employment, and logging.

Ketchikan is Alaska's totem-pole port: at the nearby Tlingit village of Saxman, 2½ mi south of downtown, there is a major totem-pole park, and residents still practice traditional carving techniques. The Ketchikan Visitors Bureau on the dock can supply information on getting to Saxman on your own, or you can take a ship-organized tour. Another excellent outdoor totem-pole display is at Totem Bight State Historical Park, a coastal rain forest 10 mi north of town. The Totem Heritage Center preserves historic poles, some nearly 200 years old.

Expect rain at some time during the day, even if the sun is shining when you dock: the average annual precipitation is more than 150 inches.

Coming Ashore

Ships dock or tender passengers ashore directly across from the **Ketchikan Visitors Bureau** (tel. 907/225–6166 or 800/770–3300) on Front and Mission streets, in the center of downtown. Most of the town's sights are within easy walking distance of downtown. You can follow the walking-tour signs that lead you around the city. For panoramic vistas of the surrounding area, climb the stairs leading up several different steep hillsides.

To reach sights farther from downtown, hire a cab or ride the local buses. Metered taxis meet the ships right on the docks and also wait across the street. Rates are $2.65 for pickup, plus 25¢ each ⅒ mi. Local buses run along on the main route through town and south to Saxman. The fare is $1.50.

Exploring Ketchikan

Numbers in the margin correspond to points of interest on the Ketchikan map.

❶ The helpful **Ketchikan Visitors Bureau** is right next to the cruise-ship docks and is filled with booths staffed by day-tour, flightseeing, and boat-tour operators. *131 Front St., tel. 907/225–6166 or 800/770–3300, www.visit-ketchikan.com. Open daily 7–6.*

❷ The impressive **Southeast Alaska Discovery Center** has museum-quality exhibits on Native culture, wildlife, logging, recreation, and the use of public lands. You can also watch its award-winning film *Mystical Southeast Alaska. 50 Main St., tel. 907/228–6220, www.nps.gov/aplic. Admission: $5. Open daily 8:30–4:30.*

You can learn about Ketchikan's rich Native culture and its early days as a fishing, mining, and logging town at the ❸ **Tongass Historical Museum.** *In library building at Dock and Bawden Sts., tel. 907/225–5600. Admission: $2. Open daily 8–5.*

For a great view of the harbor, take curving Venetia Avenue to the **West Coast Cape Fox Lodge.** Not only are the ❹

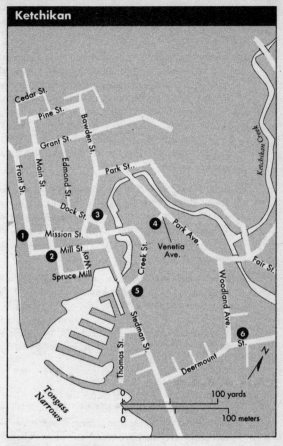

Ketchikan

Cedar St.
Pine St.
Bawden St.
Grant St.
Edmond St.
Main St.
Front St.
Park St.
Dock St.
Mission St.
Mill St.
No 2
Spruce Mill
Creek St.
Park Ave
Venetia Ave.
Fair St.
Woodland Ave.
Stedman St.
Thomas St.
Deermount
Ketchikan Creek
Tongass Narrows

100 yards
0
0
100 meters

Creek Street 5

Ketchikan Visitors Bureau 1

Southeast Alaska Discovery Center 2

Tongass Historical Museum 3

Totem Heritage Center 6

West Coast Cape Fox Lodge 4

views stunning but the dining is excellent. You can also take a short funicular car ride ($1) up the hillside from Creek Street.

❺ Creek Street, formerly Ketchikan's infamous red-light district, is the picturesque centerpiece of town. Its small houses, built on stilts over the creek, have been restored as trendy shops. There's good salmon viewing in season at the Creek Street footbridge. The street's most famous brothel, **Dolly's House** (tel. 907/225–6329; admission $4), has been preserved as a museum, complete with original furnishings and a short history of the life and times of Ketchikan's best-known madam.

❻ Every visitor to Ketchikan should stop by the **Totem Heritage Center,** which has a fascinating display of weathered, original totem carvings, some more than a century old. *Woodland Ave. at corner of Deermont St., tel. 907/225–5900. Admission: May.–Sept $4, Oct.–Apr. free. Open daily 8–5.*

Most local bus tours take in **Totem Bight State Historical Park,** on a pretty point of land 10 mi north of Ketchikan. Here you will find 15 totems (most from the 1930s) and a clan house facing Tongass Narrows. Tour buses (or taxis) also head south from Ketchikan 2½ mi to the village of **Saxman,** where many more totems are located around a modern clan house.

Shopping

Because artists are local, prices for Native Alaskan crafts are sometimes lower in Ketchikan than at other ports. The **Saxman Village** gift shop has some Tlingit wares along with less expensive mass-produced souvenirs. A better bet is to head a block downhill to **Saxman Arts Co-op** (tel. 907/225–4166), where the baskets, button blankets (traditional wool blankets, usually bright red, with designs made from ivory-colored buttons sewn into the fabric), moccasins, wood carvings, and jewelry are all locally made.

AlaskaMade Gallery (123 Stedman St., tel. 907/225–5404 or 888/877–9706) has locally crafted pieces. **Creek Street** has several attractive boutiques. At **Parnassus Bookstore** (5 Creek St., tel. 907/225–7690), you can browse through an eclectic collection of books. The same building houses

Soho Coho Contemporary Art and Craft Gallery (tel. 907/225–5954 or 800/888–4070), headquarters for artist Ray Troll, Alaska's well-known producer of all things weird and fishy.

Salmon, Etc. (322 Mission St., tel. 907/225–6008 or 800/354–7256) sells canned, smoked, or frozen salmon and other Alaskan seafood and will be happy to ship your purchase.

Outdoor Activities and Sports

FISHING

Salmon are so plentiful in these waters that the town has earned the nickname Salmon Capital of the World. The **Ketchikan Visitors Bureau** (131 Front St., 99901, tel. 907/225–6166 or 800/770–3300, www.visit-ketchikan.com) has a full list of charter companies, or sign up for a sportfishing adventure at your shore-excursion desk.

HIKING

Check at the visitor's bureau on the dock for trail maps and advice. If you're a tough hiker with sturdy waterproof boots and rain gear, the trail from downtown (starting at the end of Fair Street) to the top of 3,000-foot **Deer Mountain** will repay your effort with a spectacular panorama of the city below and the wilderness behind. It's 6 mi roundtrip and will probably take you several hours. The **Ward Lake Area,** about 6 mi north of town, offers easier hiking along lakes and streams and beneath towering spruce and hemlock trees. The **Southeast Alaska Discovery Center** (50 Main St., tel. 907/228–6220, www.nps.gov/aplic) has trail maps detailing these and other U.S. Forest Service trails.

KAYAKING AND CANOEING

Southeast Exposure (tel. 907/225–8829, www.southeastexposure.com) rents kayaks and mountain bikes and guides kayaking trips. **Southeast Sea Kayaks** (tel. 907/225–1258 or 800/287–1607, www.kayakketchikan.com) leads tours of Ketchikan's historic waterfront and provides kayak rentals, along with guided trips to Misty Fiords.

Dining

$$–$$$$ ✕ **Annabelle's Keg and Chowder House.** Housed within the historic Gilmore Hotel, this seafood restaurant takes you back to the 1920s. The walls are covered with photos and paintings depicting the Ketchikan of years past. Spe-

cials include clams, oysters on the half shell, delicious seafood chowders, prime rib, and pasta. Afterward, be sure to order a slice of peanut-butter pie. *326 Front St., tel. 907/225–6009. AE, D, DC, MC, V.*

$$–$$$$ ✕ **Steamers.** This spacious and lively restaurant in the Spruce Mill Mall has tall windows facing Ketchikan's busy waterfront, where cruise ships and floatplanes vie for your attention. Menu specials include seafood of all types, and the bar pours 19 draft beers (including a number of Alaskan brews), along with a substantial wine list and 300 different liquors. *76 Front St., tel. 907/225–1600. AE, D, DC, MC, V.*

Saloons

There's no pretense of formality at the **Potlatch Bar** (tel. 907/225–4855) in Thomas Basin, where local fisherfolk and cannery workers play pool and tip back cans of Rainier beer.

Kodiak Island

The second-largest island in the United States (Hawaii's Big Island is the largest), Kodiak is an out-of-the-way destination for smaller cruise ships and Alaska state ferries. Russian explorers discovered the island in 1763, and Kodiak served as Alaska's first capital until 1804, when the government was moved to Sitka. Situated as it is in the northwestern Gulf of Alaska, Kodiak has been subjected to several natural disasters. In 1912 a volcanic eruption on the nearby Alaska Peninsula covered the town site in knee-deep drifts of ash and pumice. A tidal wave resulting from the 1964 earthquake destroyed the island's large fishing fleet and smashed Kodiak's low-lying downtown area.

Today commercial fishing is king in Kodiak. Despite its small population—about 15,000 people scattered among the several islands in the Kodiak group—the city is among the busiest fishing ports in the United States. The harbor is also an important supply point for small communities on the Aleutian Islands and the Alaska Peninsula. Kodiak weather is notorious, with rain being the predominant feature much of the time, but when the sun shines it's hard to imagine a more beautiful setting.

Coming Ashore

Most cruise ships dock at Pier 2, ½ mi south of downtown Kodiak. Some ships offer shuttles into town, but if yours does not, it's a 15-minute walk. You can catch a cab ride from **A&B Taxi** (tel. 907/486–4343) for $6.

Pick up maps, details on kayaking trips, bear-viewing flights, marine tours, and more from the downtown visitor center, which is staffed whenever cruise ships are in port.

Exploring Kodiak

One of the chief attractions in the area is the 1.6-million-acre **Kodiak National Wildlife Refuge,** which lies partly on Kodiak Island and partly on Afognak Island to the north and where spotting the enormous Kodiak brown bears is the main goal of a trip. Seeing the Kodiak brown bears, which weigh a pound at birth but up to 1,500 pounds when fully grown, is worth the trip to this rugged country. The bears are spotted easily in July and August, feeding along salmon-spawning streams. Charter flightseeing trips are available to the area, and exaggerated tales of encounters with these impressive beasts are frequently heard. *1390 Buskin River Rd., Kodiak 99615, tel. 907/487–2600, www.r7.fws.gov/nwr/kodiak.*

As part of America's North Pacific defense in World War II, Kodiak was the site of an important naval station, now occupied by the Coast Guard fleet that patrols the surrounding fishing grounds. Part of the old military installation has been incorporated into **Fort Abercrombie State Park,** 3½ mi north of Kodiak on Rezanof Drive. The land is carpeted with spruce trees and trails lead past old concrete bunkers and gun emplacements to magnificent shores. You'll even see nesting puffins on the cliffs here. *tel. 907/486–6339, www.dnr.state.ak.us/parks.*

The **Baranof Museum** presents artifacts from the area's Russian origins. Built in 1808 by Alexander Baranof to warehouse precious sea-otter pelts, the museum is in one of the oldest Russian buildings in North America. On display are samovars, Russian Easter eggs, Native baskets, and other relics from the early Native Koniags and the later Russian settlers. *101 Marine Way, tel. 907/486–5920, ☞ $2. Open daily 10–4.*

The ornate **Holy Resurrection Russian Orthodox Church** is a visual feast, both inside and out. The cross-shape building is topped by two onion-shape blue domes, and the interior contains brass candle stands, distinctive chandeliers, and numerous icons representing Orthodox saints. Three different churches have stood on this site since 1794. Built in 1945, the present structure is on the National Register of Historic Places. *Corner of Mission and Kashevaroff Rds., tel. 907/486–3854 (parish priest). By appointment.*

The **Alutiiq Museum** is home to one of the largest collections of Eskimo materials in the world and contains archaeological and ethnographic items dating back 7,500 years. Museum displays include harpoons, masks, dolls, stone tools, seal-gut parkas, grass baskets, and pottery fragments. The museum store sells Native arts. *215 Mission Rd., Suite 101, tel. 907/486–7004, www.alutiiqmuseum.com. Admission: $2. Open weekdays 9–5, Sat. 10–5, Sun. by appointment.*

Guided Tours

Kodiak Island Charters (tel. 907/486–5380 or 800/575–5380, www.ptialaska.net/~urascal) operates boat tours for fishing and sightseeing. It'll take you on a combined halibut and salmon trip, with sightseeing and whale-watching thrown in as well. **Kodiak Tours** (tel. 907/486–3920, www.kodiaktours.com) has van tours of historical sites in Kodiak, including cannery row, the Russian Orthodox church, Alutiiq Museum, and Baranof Museum.

Dining

$–$$$$ ╳ **Henry's Great Alaskan Restaurant.** Henry's is a boisterous, friendly, and smoky downtown spot. The menu is the biggest in town and ranges from fresh local seafood to barbecue to pastas and even some Cajun dishes. A long list of appetizers, salads, and tasty desserts rounds out the choices. The bar is popular with sports enthusiasts. *512 Marine Way, tel. 907/486–8844. AE, MC, V.*

$$ ╳ **El Chicano.** This unexpectedly authentic Mexican restaurant dishes up all the traditional favorites, from chiles rellenos to homemade tamales. There are large servings at reasonable prices. *103 Center St., tel. 907/486–6116. AE, D, MC, V.*

$ ✕ **Monk's Rock Coffee House.** Run by the St. Herman of Alaska Brotherhood, a splinter group of the Russian Orthodox Church, this unusual little gathering spot is a pleasant place for coffee, tea, smoothies, fresh-squeezed juices, and ice cream. Books are for sale, and the back room doubles as a chapel. *202 E. Rezanof Dr., tel. 907/486–0905. No credit cards.*

Metlakatla

The village of Metlakatla is on Annette Island, just a dozen miles from busy Ketchikan but a world away culturally. A visit to this quiet and conservative place offers the chance to learn about life in a small Inside Passage Native community. Local taxis can take you to other sights around the island, including Yellow Hill and the old air force base.

In most Southeast Native villages, the people are Tlingit or Haida in heritage. Metlakatla is the exception: here most folks are Tsimshian. They moved to the island from British Columbia in 1887, led by William Duncan, an Anglican missionary from England. The new town grew rapidly and soon included dozens of buildings laid out on a grid of streets—a cannery, a sawmill, and a church that could seat 1,000 people. Congress declared Annette Island a federal Indian reservation in 1891, and it remains the only reservation in Alaska today. Father Duncan continued to control life in Metlakatla for decades, until the government finally stepped in shortly before his death in 1918.

During World War II the U.S. Army built a major air base 7 mi from Metlakatla that included observation towers for Japanese subs, airplane hangars, gun emplacements, and housing for 10,000 soldiers. After the war it served as Ketchikan's airport for many years, but today the long runways are virtually abandoned save for a few private flights.

Coming Ashore
Cruise ships dock at the Metlakatla dock adjacent to town. Buses from **Metlakatla Tours** (tel. 907/886–8687, tours. metlakatla.net) meet all ships.

Exploring Metlakatla

Metlakatla's religious heritage still shows through today. The clapboard **William Duncan Memorial Church,** topped with two steeples, burned in 1948 but was rebuilt several years later. It is one of nine churches in tiny Metlakatla. **Father Duncan's Cottage** is maintained as it was when he was alive and includes numerous artifacts, personal items, and historic photographs. *Corner of 4th Ave. and Church St., tel. 907/886–8687. Admission: $2. Open when cruise ships are in port.*

Father Duncan worked hard to eliminate traditional Tsimshian beliefs and dances, so he would probably not approve of recent efforts to relearn the old ways. Today the people of Metlakatla proudly perform these old dances and stories. The best place to see this is at the traditional **longhouse,** which faces Metlakatla's boat harbor. Three totem poles stand on the back side of the building, and the front is covered with a Tsimshian design. Inside are displays of Native crafts and a model of the fish traps that were once common throughout the Inside Passage. Just down from the longhouse is an **Artists' Village,** where booths display locally made arts and crafts. The village and longhouse open when groups and tours are present.

Guided Tours

Run by the Metlakatla Indian community, **Metlakatla Tours** (tel. 907/886–8687, tours.metlakatla.net) leads bus tours that include visits to Father Duncan's Cottage, the cannery, and the longhouse, along with a Tsimshian dance performance.

Dining

$$ ✕ **Metlakatla Hotel and Restaurant.** The restaurant here is open for lunch and dinner and has the usual American favorites, along with fresh seafood. *3rd Ave. and Lower Milton St., tel. 907/886–3456. AE, D, MC, V.*

Misty Fiords National Monument

In the past, cruise ships bypassed Misty Fiords on their way up and down the Inside Passage. But today more and more cruise passengers are discovering its unspoiled beauty as ships big and small feature a day of scenic cruising through this protected wilderness. At the southern end of the Inside Passage, Misty Fiords usually lies just before or after a call at Ketchikan. The attraction here is the wilderness—3,500 square mi of it—highlighted by waterfalls and cliffs that rise 3,000 ft. If your ship doesn't visit here, consider taking a tour of the area with **Alaska Cruises** (tel. 907/225–6044 or 800/228–1905, www.goldbelttours.com) when you visit nearby Ketchikan.

Nome

One of the most remote cruise-ship destinations, Nome is visited by Cruise West adventure ships as part of their Bering Sea trips, which include Homer, Kodiak, Dutch Harbor, the Pribilofs, and Siberia. More than a century has passed since a great stampede for gold put a speck of wilderness called Nome on the Alaska map, but gold mining and noisy saloons are still mainstays in this frontier community on the icy Bering Sea. Only 165 mi from the coast of Siberia, Nome is considerably closer to Russia than either Anchorage or Fairbanks. And though you'll find a local road system, to get to Nome you must either fly or mush a team of sled dogs. Mainly a collection of ramshackle houses and low-slung commercial buildings, Nome looks like a vintage gold-mining camp or the neglected set of a western movie—raw-boned, rugged, and somewhat shabby. What the town lacks in appearance is made up for with a cheerful hospitality and colorful history.

Nome's golden years began in 1898, when three prospectors—known as the Lucky Swedes—struck rich deposits on Anvil Creek, about 4 mi from what became Nome. The news spread quickly. When the Bering Sea ice parted the next spring, ships from Puget Sound, down by Seattle, arrived in Nome with eager stampeders. An estimated 15,000 people landed in Nome between June and October of 1900. Among the gold-rush luminaries were Wyatt Earp, the old gunfighter from the O.K. Corral, who mined the gold of Nome by opening a posh saloon; Tex Rickard, the boxing promoter, who operated another Nome saloon; and Rex Beach, the novelist.

A network of 250 mi or so of gravel roads around the town leads to creeks and rivers for gold panning or fishing for trout, salmon, and arctic grayling. You can also see reindeer, bears, foxes, and moose in the wild on the back roads that once connected early mining camps and hamlets.

Coming Ashore

Cruise ships dock a mile south of Nome at the city dock. Taxis are available to downtown for $5. Most travelers take a tour of the area through either **Nome Discovery Tours** (tel. 907/443–2814) or **Nome Tour and Marketing** (tel. 907/443–2651).

Exploring Nome

For exploring downtown, stop at the **Nome Convention and Visitors Bureau** (301 Front St., tel. 907/443–6624, 800/478–1901 in Alaska, www.nomealaska.org/vc) for a historic-walking-tour map, a city map, and information on local activities from flightseeing to bird-watching.

Shopping

Nome is one of the best places to buy ivory, because many of the Eskimo carvers from outlying villages come to Nome first to offer their wares to dealers. The Marine Mammals Protection Act permits the purchase of walrus-ivory goods from Native Alaskans. The **Arctic Trading Post** (Bering and Front Sts., tel. 907/443–2686) has an extensive stock of authentic Eskimo ivory carvings and other Alaskan artwork, jewelry, and books. The **Board of Trade Ivory Shop** (211 Front St., tel. 907/443–2611) specializes in ivory carvings but also sells Native Alaskan artwork and handicrafts. **Chukotka–Alaska** (514 Lomen Ave., tel. 907/443–4128 or 800/416–4128) sells both Native Alaskan and Russian artwork and handicrafts as well as books, beads, and furs.

Dining

$$–$$$$ ✕ **Fort Davis Roadhouse.** Specializing in prime rib and seafood, the Roadhouse is where locals go for a night out or Sunday brunch. Above the dining area is a lounge with live music and room for dancing. Taxis serve the area. *Nome–Council Rd., 1½ mi east of town, tel. 907/443–2660. MC, V.*

$–$$$ ✕ **Fat Freddie's.** This popular family-style eatery overlooking the Bering Sea serves New York steak and prime rib, plus notable burgers and chowder. *50 Front St., tel. 907/443–5899. AE, D, MC, V.*

Saloons

Since its establishment more than a century ago, Nome has always been a place where drinking is a major focus. Because all the surrounding Native villages are dry, many folks come here to drink to excess. The town's most famous bar is **Board of Trade Saloon** (211 Front St., tel. 907/443–2611), which was originally owned by Wyatt Earp (when it was called the Dexter Saloon).

Petersburg

Getting to Petersburg is a heart-quickening experience. Only ferries and the smallest cruise ships can squeak through Wrangell Narrows, with the aid of more than 50 buoys and markers along the 22-mi (35-km) crossing. The inaccessibility of Petersburg is part of its charm. And unlike several other Southeast communities, this one is never overwhelmed with hordes of cruise passengers.

At your first glimpse of Petersburg you may think you're in old Norway. Neat, white Scandinavian-style homes and storefronts with steep roofs and decorated with bright-colored swirls of leaf-and-flower designs (called rosemaling) and row upon row of sturdy fishing vessels in the harbor invoke the spirit of Norway. No wonder—this prosperous fishing community was founded by Norwegian Peter Buschmann in 1897.

The Little Norway Festival is held here each year on the third full weekend in May. If you're in town during the festival, be sure to take part in one of the fish feeds. The beer-batter halibut is delectable, and you won't find better folk dancing outside of Norway.

Coming Ashore

Ships that are small enough to visit Petersburg dock in the South Harbor, which is about a ½-mi (1-km) walk from downtown. Everything in Petersburg, including the **Petersburg Visitor Information Center** (tel. 907/772–4636, www.petersburg.org) on 1st and Fram streets, is also within easy walking distance of the harbor.

Renting a bicycle is an especially pleasant way to see the sights. Ride along the coast on Nordic Drive, past the lovely homes, to the boardwalk and the city dump, where you might spot some bears. Coming back to town, take the interior route and you'll pass the airport and some pretty churches before returning to the waterfront. Bikes are available from **Petersburg Bicycle Rentals** (1216 S. Nordic Dr., tel. 907/772–3929).

If you want to learn about the local history, the commercial fishing industry, and the Tongass National Forest, you can take a guided tour. **Viking Travel** (tel. 907/772–3818) books whale-watching, glacier-viewing, sea-kayaking, and other charters with local operators.

Exploring Petersburg

Numbers in the margin correspond to points of interest on the Petersburg map.

One of the most pleasant things to do in Petersburg is to roam among the fishing vessels tied up at dockside. This is one of Alaska's busiest, most prosperous fishing communities, and the variety of boats is enormous. You'll see small trollers, big halibut vessels, and sleek pleasure craft as well. Wander, too, around the fish-processing structures (though beware of the pungent aroma). Just by watching shrimp, salmon, or halibut catches being brought ashore, you can get a real appreciation for this industry and the people who engage in it.

The peaks of the Coastal Range behind the town mark the border between Canada and the United States; the most striking is **Devils Thumb,** at 9,077 ft. About 25 mi east of Petersburg lies spectacular **LeConte Glacier,** the continent's southernmost tidewater glacier and one of its most active ones. It often happens that so many icebergs have calved into the bay that the entrance is carpeted bank to bank with the floating bergs. The glacier is accessible only by water or air; contact **Kaleidoscope Cruises** (tel. 907/772–3736 or 800/868–4373, www.alaska.net/~bbsea) to schedule a five-hour trip.

❶ For a scenic hike closer to town, go north 3 mi on Nordic Drive to **Sandy Beach,** one of Petersburg's favorite spots for picnics and recreation and good eagle-viewing.

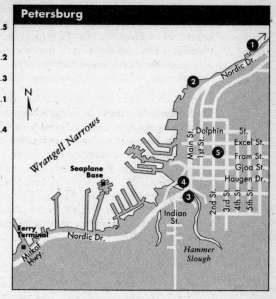

The best place to watch for America's national bird is the appropriately named **Eagle's Roost Park,** along the shore north of the Petersburg Fisheries cannery. At low tide you may see more than two dozen eagles diving for live fish or carrion here.

Back in the center of town, stop at **Hammer Slough,** a narrow inlet lined with weathered houses built on stilts, which makes for a postcard-perfect picture. At high tide, the slough fills with saltwater and measures 100 ft bank to bank. The large, white, barnlike structure that borders the slough is the **Sons of Norway Hall,** where descendants of Norwegian settlers keep the traditions and culture of the old country alive.

At 2nd and Fram streets you'll find the **Clausen Memorial Museum** and the bronze *Fisk* (Norwegian for "fish") sculpture. Not surprisingly, the museum devotes a lot of its space to fishing and fish processing. There's an old "iron chink," used in the early days for gutting and cleaning fish, as well as displays on several types of fishing boats. On exhibit are a 126½-pound king salmon, the largest ever caught, which came out of a fish trap on Prince of Wales Island in 1939, and the world's largest chum salmon—a 36-pounder. *203 Fram St., tel. 907/772–3598, www. clausenmuseum.alaska.net. Admission: $2. Open Mon.–Sat. 10:30–4:30.*

Three **pioneer churches**—Catholic, Lutheran, and Presbyterian—are nearby at Dolphin and 3rd streets, Excel and 5th streets, and on Haugen Street between 2nd and 3rd streets, respectively. Of the three, the 50-year-old Lutheran church is the oldest. It is said that boys would bring dirt loads by the wheelbarrow for landscaping around the foundation. Their compensation? Ice cream cones. The enticement was so successful that, after three years of ice cream rewards, it was necessary to bring in a bulldozer to scrape off the excess dirt.

Shopping

One of the Southeast's gourmet delicacies is Petersburg pink salad shrimp. Small (they're seldom larger than half your pinky finger), tender, and succulent, they're much treasured by Alaskans, who often send them "outside" as thank-you gifts. You'll find the little critters fresh in meat departments and canned in gift sections at food stores throughout the Panhandle. You can buy fresh vacuum-packed Petersburg shrimp at **Coastal Cold Storage Fish Market** (306 N. Nordic Dr. tel. 907/772–4177) downtown, or by mail order.

At **Tonka Seafoods** (Sing Lee Alley, tel. 907/772–3662 or 888/560–3662, www.tonkaseafoods.com. Admission: Free. Open Mon.–Sat. 8–5; tours at 1 PM [minimum 6 people].), across the street from the Sons of Norway Hall, you can tour the plant and sample smoked or canned halibut and salmon.

Dining

$–$$ ✕ **Alaskafe.** The café serves panini sandwiches, homemade soups, salads, pastas, desserts, and coffee all day. The outdoor balcony seats are nice on a sunny day. *Upstairs at corner of Nordic and Excel Sts., tel. 907/772–5282. No credit cards.*

$ ✕ Coastal Cold Storage Fish Market. This is the place to
go in Petersburg for fresh seafood. Although primarily a
lunch spot, it is also open for breakfast and dinner, with
fish chowders, beer-batter halibut, shrimp cocktail, and sandwiches. It will also ship fresh, smoked, canned, or frozen
fish or process any that you catch. *306 N. Nordic Dr., tel.
907/772–4171. D, DC, MC, V.*

Saloons

The **Harbor Bar** (Nordic Dr. near Dolphin St., tel. 907/772–
4526), with ship's wheels, ship pictures, and a mounted red
snapper, is true to the town's seafaring spirit.

A colorful, authentic Alaskan bar of regional fame, **Kito's
Kave** (Sing Lee Alley, tel. 907/772–3207) serves Mexican
food in a smoky, pool-hall atmosphere. It's not for the
timid or faint of heart.

Prince Rupert, British Columbia

The port of Prince Rupert is the largest community on
British Columbia's north coast. Set on Kaien Island at the
mouth of the Skeena River and surrounded by deep green
fjords and coastal rain forest, Prince Rupert is rich in the
culture of the Tsimshian, people who have been in the area
for thousands of years.

As the western terminus of Canada's second transcontinental
railroad and blessed with a deep natural harbor, Prince
Rupert was, at the time of its incorporation in 1910, poised
to rival Vancouver as a center for trans-Pacific trade. This
didn't happen, partly because the main visionary behind
the scheme, Grand Trunk Pacific Railroad president Charles
Hays, went down with the *Titanic* on his way back from
a financing trip to England. Prince Rupert turned instead
to fishing and forestry. New to hosting cruise ships, this community of 14,000 retains a laid-back, small-town air.

Besides the attractions detailed below, some shore excursions worth joining if they're available are half-day train
trips into Prince Rupert's mountainous hinterland and any
of the First Nations cultural tours offered by local Tsimshian
guides.

Coming Ashore

Ocean liners calling at Prince Rupert dock at the **Northland Cruise Ship Terminal**, just steps from the Museum of Northern British Columbia and a few blocks from either downtown or the historic Cow Bay district. Smaller vessels tie up at **Atlin Cruise Ship Terminal** at Cow Bay. The terminals for both British Columbia and Alaska ferries as well as the VIA Rail train station are grouped together about 2 km (1 mi) from town.

Most points of interest are within walking distance of either cruise-ship terminal. **BC Transit** (tel. 250/624–6400) buses have service around town. For a taxi, contact **Skeena Taxi** (tel. 250/624–2185).

Exploring Prince Rupert

Cow Bay, a five-minute walk from the main cruise-ship terminal, is a historic waterfront area of shops, galleries, seafood restaurants, and fishing boats. Cow Bay takes its name seriously: lamp posts, benches, and anything else stationary is painted Holstein-style. While here, you can stop for a coffee at Cowpuccino's, shop for local crafts, or take a kayak tour to explore the nearby wilderness. Prince Rupert's **Visitor Information Centre** (tel. 250/624–5637 or 800/667–1994) is at Atlin Terminal in Cow Bay.

The **Museum of Northern British Columbia,** in a longhouse-style facility overlooking the waterfront, has one of the province's finest collections of coastal First Nations art, with some artifacts that date back 10,000 years. Artisans work on totem poles in the carving shed, and in summer museum staff run walking tours of the town. The museum also operates the **Kwinista Railway Museum,** a five-minute walk away on the waterfront. *100 1st Ave. W, tel. 250/624–3207, www.museumofnorthernbc.com. Admission: $5. Open Oct.–mid-May, Mon.–Sat. 9–5; mid-May–Aug., Mon.–Sat. 9–8, Sun. 9–5; Sept., daily 9–5.*

In the late 19th century, hundreds of cannery villages, built on pilings on the edge of the wilderness, lined the coast between California and Alaska. Most are gone now, but B.C.'s oldest (it dates to 1889) and most complete is the **North Pacific Historic Fishing Village** in Port Edward, 20 km (12 mi) south of Prince Rupert at the mouth of the Skeena

River. Once home to more than 700 people during each canning season, the town, including managers' houses, the company store, and cannery works, is now a national historic site. Staff lead tours and demonstrations about fishing methods, the canning process, and the unique culture of cannery villages. A one-man play about the area's history runs at least daily. The site also has a seafood restaurant and overnight accommodation. If you haven't booked a shore excursion, you can catch a B.C. Transit bus here from Cow Bay. *Off Hwy. 16, Port Edward, tel. 250/628–3538, www.district.portedward.bc.ca/northpacific. Admission: $12. Open May–Sept., daily 9–6.*

Shopping
The **Blue Heron Gallery** (123 Cow Bay Rd., tel. 250/624–5700) has Northwest Coast First Nations art and work by other local artists. The **Cow Bay Gift Galley** (24 Cow Bay Rd., tel. 250/627—1808) has gifts, souvenirs, and local art.

Outdoor Activities and Sports
Eco-Treks Adventures (203 Cow Bay Rd., tel. 250/624–8311, www.citytel.net/ecotreks) has kayak rentals and kayaking as well as Zodiac tours (one- and multiday) of nearby fjords and islands. Many of the trips are suitable for beginners.

Dining
$–$$ ✕ **Cow Bay Cafe.** Fresh, local seafood and creative vegetarian dishes shine at this tiny waterfront café, where the friendly chef-owner makes almost everything (including breads and desserts) from scratch. What's on the chalkboard menu depends on what's fresh that day but could include curries, Mexican dishes, or the popular crab cakes. The bright solariumlike room with floor-to-ceiling ocean-view windows only seats 35, so reservations are highly recommended. *205 Cow Bay Rd., tel. 250/627–1212. AE, MC, V. Closed Sun. and Mon. No dinner Tues.*

Prince William Sound

Every Gulf of Alaska cruise visits Prince William Sound. The sound made worldwide headlines in 1989, when the *Exxon Valdez* hit a reef and spilled 11 million gallons of North Slope crude. Vast sections of the sound appear pristine today, with abundant wildlife, but the oil has sunk into the beaches below the surface. The lasting effects on the area of this lurking oil—sometimes uncovered after storms and high tides—are still being studied.

Exploring Prince William Sound

Numbers in the margin correspond to points of interest on the South Central Alaska map.

❶ A visit to **Columbia Glacier,** which flows from the surrounding Chugach Mountains, is included on many Gulf of Alaska cruises. Its deep aquamarine face is 5 mi across, and it calves new icebergs with resounding cannonades. This glacier is one of the largest and most readily accessible of Alaska's coastal glaciers.

❷ The major attraction in Prince William Sound on most Gulf of Alaska cruises is the day spent in **College Fjord.** Dubbed "Alaska's newest Glacier Bay" by one cruise line, this deep finger of water is ringed by 16 glaciers, each named after one of the colleges that sponsored early exploration of the fjord.

❸ The three largest Prince William Sound communities— Valdez, Whittier, and Cordova—are all visited by cruise ships, but none are major destinations. **Valdez** (pronounced val-*deez*) is a popular port of call for cruise ships, and Whittier has replaced Seward as a terminus for Princess cruises, but Cordova is visited only by the smaller, expedition-style cruise ships.

Seward

On the southeastern coast of the Kenai Peninsula, Seward is surrounded by four major federal landholdings—**Chugach National Forest, Kenai Wildlife Refuge, Kenai Fjords National Park,** and the **Alaska Maritime National Wildlife Refuge.** The entire area is breathtaking, and you should not miss it in your haste to get to Anchorage. Although many cruise ships stop in Seward, travelers are often shunted onto waiting buses or train cars with no time to explore this lovely town. Try to make sure that your itinerary includes time spent in the city itself.

Seward is one of Alaska's oldest and most scenic communities, set between high mountain ranges on one side and

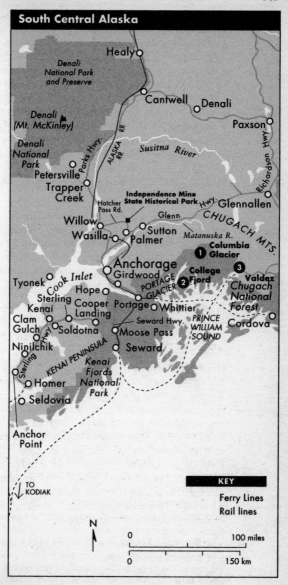

South Central Alaska

Healy

Denali National Park and Preserve

Cantwell

Denali

Paxson

Denali (Mt. McKinley)

Denali National Park

Susitna River

Petersville

Trapper Creek

ALASKA RR

Parks Hwy.

Richardson Hwy

Hatcher Pass Rd.

Independence Mine State Historical Park

Glennallen

Willow

Glenn

CHUGACH MTS.

Wasilla

Palmer

Sutton

Matanuska R.

Glenn Hwy.

1 **Columbia Glacier**

Anchorage

3

Girdwood

College Fiord

Tyonek

Cook Inlet

PORTAGE GLACIER

2

Valdez

Hope

Sterling

Cooper Landing

Portage

Whittier

Chugach National Forest

Kenai

Clam Gulch

Soldotna

Seward Hwy.

PRINCE WILLIAM SOUND

Cordova

Ninilchik

Sterling Hwy

KENAI PENINSULA

Moose Pass

Seward

Kenai Fjords National Park

Homer

Seldovia

Anchor Point

TO KODIAK

N

KEY

Ferry Lines

Rail lines

0   100 miles

0   150 km

Resurrection Bay on the other. The city was named for U.S. Secretary of State William H. Seward, who was instrumental in arranging the purchase of Alaska from Russia in 1867. Resurrection Bay was named in 1791 by Russian fur trader and explorer Alexander Baranof. The town was established in 1903 by railroad surveyors as an ocean terminal and supply center. The biggest event in Seward's history came after the 1964 Good Friday earthquake—the strongest ever recorded in North America. The tsunami that followed the quake devastated the town; fortunately, most residents saw the harbor drain almost entirely, knew the wave would follow, and ran to high ground. Since then the town has relied heavily on commercial fishing, and its harbor is important for shipping coal to Asia.

Historic downtown Seward retains its small-town atmosphere. Many of its early 20th-century buildings survived the 1964 earthquake or were rebuilt. Modern-day explorers can enjoy wildlife cruises, sportfishing, sailing, and kayaking in the bay or investigating the intricacies of marine biology at the **Alaska SeaLife Center.**

If you're in Seward on the 4th of July, you'll have the chance to see—and perhaps join—the second-oldest footrace in North America. Each year participants race straight up 3,022-foot Mt. Marathon from downtown.

Coming Ashore

Cruise ships dock approximately ½ mi from downtown. The Seward Chamber of Commerce has a visitor information center at the cruise-ship dock that is staffed when ships are in port. The Kenai Fjords National Park visitor center (tel. 907/224–3175, Open daily 8–7) is within walking distance: turn left as you leave the pier, then left again onto 4th Avenue; the center is two blocks ahead. Ask here about visiting scenic Exit Glacier, which is 13 mi northwest of Seward. The Alaska National Historical Society operates a book and gift store in the Park Service center. The Chugach National Forest Ranger District office is at 334 4th Avenue.

The **Seward's Trolley** (tel. 907/224–8051) stops at the cruise-ship dock every half hour and heads to Seward's various points of interest. The cost is $2 per ride or $5 for the whole day.

Exploring Seward

Funded largely from the 1989 *Exxon Valdez* oil spill settlement, the **Alaska SeaLife Center** is a modern facility on a 7-acre site facing Resurrection Bay. The main attractions here are the giant aquariums where you can watch Steller sea lions, harbor seals, puffins, and other animals through large underwater windows. In addition, the SeaLife Center houses tide-pool touch-tanks and smaller aquariums filled with other sea creatures. The facility is also an important center for marine research, rehabilitation, and education. *301 Railway Ave., at end of 4th Ave., tel. 907/224–6300 or 800/224–2525, www.alaskasealife.org. Admission: $12.50. Open daily 8–8.*

A tour of Seward's scenic surrounding waters is well worth your time; look for migrating whales, sea lions, sea otters, an array of seabirds, and calving glaciers in Resurrection Bay and along the coast of the Kenai Peninsula. There are numerous tours to choose from—just check out the boardwalk area adjacent to the docks. **Kenai Fjords Tours** (tel. 907/224–8068 or 800/478–8068, www.kenaifjords.com) has a very good half-day cruise of the bay with a stop for a salmon bake on Fox Island ($125 for an eight-hour cruise). Other tour companies are **Renown Charters and Tours** (tel. 907/224–3806 or 800/655–3806, www.renowncharters.com) and **Major Marine Tours** (tel. 907/224–8030 or 800/764–7300, www.majormarine.com).

Exit Glacier, 13 mi northeast of Seward, is the only road-accessible part of Kenai Fjords National Park. It's an easy ½-mi (1-km) hike to Exit Glacier from the parking lot, the first ¼ mi of which is paved.

If you're looking for history, check out the **Seward Museum,** which has exhibits on the 1964 earthquake; the Iditarod Trail, the route of the 1925 diphtheria serum run from Seward to Nome (now commemorated by an annual 1,100-mi dogsled race); and Native history. *Corner of 3rd and Jefferson Sts., tel. 907/224–3902. Admission: $2. Open daily 9–5.*

Across from the museum is the **1916 Rail Car Seward.** Once part of the Alaska Railroad's rolling stock, it is now permanently parked here as an information center. Displays inside detail the 1964 Good Friday earthquake and how it devastated the town of Seward.

Shopping

Bardarson Studio (1317 4th Ave., tel. 907/224–5448 www.bardarsonstudio.com), selling everything from prints and watercolors to sculpture and beaded earrings, is a browser's dream. Try some of the home-baked breads, pastries, and espresso at the **Ranting Raven Bakery** (228 4th Ave., tel. 907/224–2228), which also has a gift shop with jewelry, Native crafts, and Russian imports.

Outdoor Activities and Sports

FISHING

Every August the **Seward Silver Salmon Derby** attracts hundreds of folks who compete for the $10,000 top prize. For fishing, sightseeing, and drop-off/pickup tours, contact the **Fish House** (tel. 907/224–3674 or 800/257–7760, www.thefishhouse.net), Seward's oldest and largest booking agency.

HIKING

The strenuous **Mt. Marathon** trail starts at the west end of Lowell Canyon Road and runs practically straight uphill. An easier and more convenient hike is the **Two Lakes Trail,** a loop of footpaths and bridges on the edge of town. A map is available from the **Seward Chamber of Commerce** (3rd Ave. and Jefferson St., tel. 907/224–8051, www.sewardak.org).

Dining

$$–$$$$ ╳ **Harbor Dinner Club & Lounge.** Stop at this spot in Seward's historic downtown district for solid lunch fare such as burgers, sandwiches, and clam chowder. The outside deck is a good place to dine on a sunny summer afternoon. *220 5th Ave., tel. 907/224–3012. AE, D, DC, MC, V.*

$$–$$$ ╳ **Ray's Waterfront.** When it comes to ultrafresh seafood, Ray's is the place. The walls are lined with trophy fish, and the windows front the busy harbor. It's a favorite place to grab a bite to eat while waiting for your tour boat or to relax with a cocktail as the sun goes down. The menu includes delicious mesquite-grilled salmon, plus clam chowder, crab, and other fresh-from-the-sea specialties. *Small-boat harbor, tel. 907/224–5606. AE, D, DC, MC, V.*

$–$$ ✕ **Resurrect Art Coffeehouse Gallery.** Constructed in 1916–
17, the building served for many years as a Lutheran church.
Today locals and tourists come to worship the espresso and
pastries, listen to live music and poetry, and shop for paintings, photographs, jewelry, and pottery. *320 3rd Ave., tel.
907/224–7161. No credit cards.*

Sitka

Sitka was home to Tlingit people for centuries before the
18th-century arrival of the Russians. But Sitka's protected
harbor, mild climate, and economic potential caught the attention of outsiders. Russian territorial governor Alexander Baranof saw in the island's massive timber forests raw
materials for shipbuilding, and its location suited trading
routes to California, Hawaii, and the Orient. In 1799,
Baranof established an outpost that he called Redoubt St.
Michael, 6 mi north of the present town, and moved a large
number of his Russian and Aleut sea-otter and seal hunters
there from Kodiak Island.

The Tlingits attacked Baranof's people and burned his
buildings in 1802, but Baranof returned in 1804 with
formidable strength, including shipboard cannons. He attacked the Tlingits at their fort near Indian River (site of
the present-day, 105-acre Sitka National Historical Park)
and drove them to Chichagof Island, 70 mi northwest of
Sitka. The Tlingits and Russians made peace in 1821, and
eventually the capital of Russian America was shifted from
Kodiak to Sitka.

Today Sitka is known for its beautiful setting plus some of
Southeast Alaska's most famous landmarks: the onion-
dome Russian Orthodox church; the Alaska Raptor Center, where you can come up close to ailing birds of prey;
and Sitka National Historical Park, where you can see
some of the oldest and most skillfully carved totem poles
in the state.

Coming Ashore

Only the smallest excursion vessels can dock at Sitka.
Ocean liners must drop anchor in the harbor and tender
passengers ashore near **Harrigan Centennial Hall.** You'll rec-

ognize the hall by the big Tlingit war canoe out front. Inside is the **Isabel Miller Museum** and an information desk for the **Sitka Visitors Bureau** (tel. 907/747–5940, www. sitka.org), where you can get a list of local charter-fishing operators. Sitka is hilly, but the waterfront attractions are an easy walk from the tender landing. You may, however, want to consider a taxi if you're heading all the way to the raptor center.

Exploring Sitka

Numbers in the margin correspond to points of interest on the Sitka map.

For one of the best views in town, turn left on Harbor Drive and head for **Castle Hill,** where Alaska was handed over to the United States on October 18, 1867, and where the first 49-star U.S. flag was flown, on January 3, 1959, signifying the spirit of Alaska's statehood. Take the first right off Harbor Drive; then look for the entrance to Baranof Castle Hill State Historic Site. Make a left on the paved path (it's wheelchair-accessible), which takes you to the top of the hill overlooking Crescent Harbor.

The **Sitka State Pioneers' Home,** which is hard to miss with its yellow paint and red roof, was built in 1934 as the first of several state-run retirement homes and medical-care facilities. The imposing 14-foot statue in front was modeled after an authentic pioneer, William "Skagway Bill" Fonda. It portrays a determined prospector with pack, pick, rifle, and supplies, headed for gold country. *Corner of Katlian and Lincoln Sts.*

Three old anchors, believed to be from 19th-century British ships, mark **Totem Square,** across the street from the Pioneers' Home. Notice the double-headed eagle of czarist Russia on the park's totem pole. Just up the street from the Pioneers' Home is the **Sheet'ka Kwaan Naa Kahidi Community House** (456 Katlian St., tel. 907/747–7290 or 888/ 270–8687 www.sitkatribal.com), which schedules demonstrations and performances by members of the Sitka tribe.

The most distinctive grave in the **Russian and Lutheran cemetery** marks the final resting place of Princess Maksoutoff, one of the most well-known members of the Russian royal family buried on Alaskan soil.

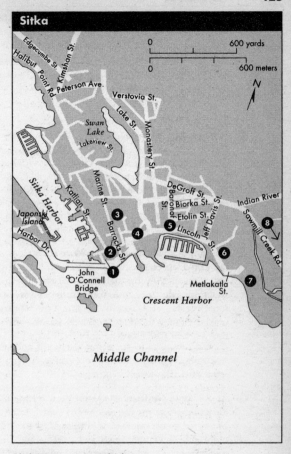

Sitka

600 yards

600 meters

N

Edgecumbe St.
Kimshan St.
Halibut Point Rd
Peterson Ave.
Verstovia St.
Lake St.
Monastery St.
Swan Lake
Lakeview St.
Sitka Harbor
Katlian St.
Marine St.
DeGroff St.
Baranof St.
Biorka St.
Etolin St.
Lincoln
Jeff Davis St.
Indian River
Sawmill Creek Rd.
Japonski Island
Harbor Dr.
Barracks St.
John O'Connell Bridge
Metlakatla St.
Crescent Harbor
Middle Channel

3 **4** **5** **8** **6** **2** **1** **7**

Alaska Raptor
Rehabilitation
Center **8**

Castle Hill . . **1**

Russian and
Lutheran
Cemetery . . . **3**

Russian
Bishop's
House **5**

St. Michael's
Cathedral . . . **4**

Sheldon
Jackson
Museum **6**

Sitka National
Historical
Park Visitor
Center **7**

Sitka State
Pioneers'
Home **2**

④ Sitka's most-photographed sight, **St. Michael's Cathedral,** was originally a frame-covered log structure built in the 1840s. In 1966 the church burned in a fire that swept through the business district. Using original blueprints, an almost exact replica of St. Michael's was built and dedicated in 1976. *Lincoln St., tel. 907/747–8120. Admission: $2. Open when cruise ships are in port.*

⑤ Several blocks past St. Michael's Cathedral on Lincoln Street and facing the harbor is the **Russian Bishop's House.** Constructed in 1842, this is one of the few remaining Russian log structures in Alaska. The Park Service has carefully restored the building, using original Russian furnishings and artifacts. In one room a portion of the house's interior has been peeled away to expose 19th-century construction techniques. *Lincoln St., tel. 907/747–6281, www.nps.gov/ sitk. Admission: $3. Open daily 9–5.*

⑥ The octagonal **Sheldon Jackson Museum,** built in 1895, contains priceless Native American items collected by Dr. Sheldon Jackson, a Presbyterian missionary and the first General Agent for Education in Alaska, during his travels to the remote regions of Alaska in the late 19th century. Carved masks, Chilkat blankets, dogsleds, kayaks—even the helmet worn by Chief Katlean during the 1804 battle between the Sitka Tlingits and the Russians—are displayed here. *104 College Dr., tel. 907/747–8981, www.museums.state.ak.us. Admission: $4. Open daily 9–5.*

⑦ At the **Sitka National Historical Park Visitor Center,** audiovisual programs and exhibits of Native and Russian artifacts tell an overview of Southeast Alaskan cultures both old and new. Native artists and craftspeople are on hand to demonstrate and interpret traditional crafts of the Tlingit people, such as silversmithing, weaving, and basket making. A self-guided forest trail (maps available at the visitor center) leading to the site of the Tlingit Fort passes by exquisitely carved totem poles; several of these 15 poles were carved for the 1904 St. Louis World's Fair. *106 Metlakatla St., tel. 907/747–6281, www.nps.gov/sitk. Admission: Free. Open daily 8–5.*

⑧ One of Sitka's most interesting attractions is the **Alaska Raptor Rehabilitation Center,** where injured bald eagles and other wild birds, such as raptors, hawks, and owls, are nursed back to health. Hiking trails crisscross the beautiful tract of land. *1101 Sawmill Creek Rd., tel. 907/747–8662 or 800/643–9425, www.alaskaraptor.org. Admission: Admission and tour $10. Open mid-May–Sept., Sun.–Fri. 8–4 and when cruise ships are in port.*

Shopping

Across the street from St. Michael's Cathedral, **Fairweather Prints** (209 Lincoln St., tel. 907/747–8677) sells beautifully printed "wearable art" with Alaskan designs. Native jewelry and other handicrafts are available from the **Sitka National Historical Park Visitor Center** (106 Metlakatla St., tel. 907/747–6281). Housed within an 1895 home, **Sitka Rose Gallery** (419 Lincoln St., tel. 907/747–3030 or 888/236–1536) has two small galleries with Alaskan paintings, sculptures, Native art, and jewelry.

Several stores, such as the **New Archangel Trading Co.** (335 Harbor Dr., across from Centennial Hall, tel. 907/747–8181) and the **Russian-American Company** (407 Lincoln St., tel. 907/747–6228) sell imported Russian items, including the popular *matryoshkas,* or nesting dolls.

Stop by **Old Harbor Books** (201 Lincoln St., tel. 907/747–8808) for photography and coffee-table books, guides and maps, fiction, poetry, and prose about Alaska or by Alaskans, as well as books on Alaska's natural history, art, and culture, both Native and contemporary.

Outdoor Activities and Sports

HIKING

Sitka's easiest hiking can be done along the 2 mi of rainforest trails in **Sitka National Historical Park.** Here you can find some of the most dramatically situated totem poles in Alaska, relax at the picnic areas, and watch spawning salmon during the summer runs on the Indian River.

SEA KAYAKING

Baidarka Boats (320 Seward St., tel. 907/747–8996, fax 907/747–4801, www.kayaksite.com) guides excellent half-day and all-day sea-kayaking trips in the Sitka area and also rents kayaks for those who want to head out on their own. Instruction is provided and no experience is necessary. Be sure to make arrangements in advance.

Dining

$$–$$$ ✕ **Bay View Restaurant.** This waterfront restaurant specializes in Russian dishes that reflect Sitka's colonial heritage. Try the borscht or the piroshkis (pierogies)—fried dumplings filled with meat and cabbage or onion. Pasta, seafood, steaks, sandwiches, and burgers are also served, as are beer and wine. *407 Lincoln St., tel. 907/747–5440. AE, MC, V.*

Saloons

Join the Sitka fisherfolk at **Pioneer Bar** (212 Katlean St., tel. 907/747–3456), across from the harbor. The walls here are lined with pictures of local fishing boats.

Skagway

The early gold-rush days of Alaska, when dreamers and hooligans descended on the Yukon via the murderous White Pass, are preserved in Skagway. Now a part of the Klondike Gold Rush National Historical Park, downtown Skagway was once the pretty but sometimes lawless gateway for the frenzied stampede to the interior goldfields.

Local park rangers and residents now interpret and re-create that remarkable era for visitors. Old false-front stores, saloons, brothels, and wood sidewalks have been completely restored. You'll be regaled with tall tales of con artists, golden-hearted "ladies," stampeders, and newsmen. Such colorful characters as outlaw Jefferson "Soapy" Smith and his gang earned the town a reputation so bad that, by the spring of 1898, the superintendent of the Northwest Royal Mounted Police had labeled Skagway "little better than a hell on earth." But Soapy was killed in a duel with surveyor Frank Reid, and soon a civilizing influence, in the form of churches and family life, prevailed. When the gold played out just a few years later, the town of 20,000 dwindled to its current population of 800 (twice that in the summer months).

Coming Ashore

Skagway is a major stop for cruise ships in Alaska, and this little town sometimes has four large ships in port at once. Some dock just a short stroll from downtown, others ¼ mi away at the Railroad Dock, where **city buses** are waiting to provide transportation to the center of town, the Gold Rush Cemetery, and other sites north of Skagway. The charge is $2 one-way in town or $5 round-trip for points north of town.

Virtually all the shops and gold-rush sights are along Broadway, the main strip that leads from the visitor center through the middle of town. It's a nice walk from the docks up through Broadway, but you can also take tours with horse-drawn surreys, antique limousines, and modern vans.

Exploring Skagway

Numbers in the margin correspond to points of interest on the Skagway map.

Skagway is perhaps the easiest port in Alaska to explore on foot. Just walk up and down Broadway, detouring here and there into the side streets. Keep an eye out for the humorous architectural details and advertising irreverence that mark the Skagway spirit.

From the pier you can see the large maroon-and-yellow building that houses the **Klondike Gold Rush National Historical Park Visitor Center** (tel. 907/983–2921, www.nps.gov/klgo; open daily 8–8). Step inside to view the historical photographs and a fine documentary video. Rangers lead guided walks through town and can provide details on nearby hiking trails (including the famous Chilkoot Trail).

Next door to the visitor center is the **White Pass & Yukon Route Depot,** the departure point for the most popular Skagway-based excursion.

Across Broadway on 2nd Avenue is a small, almost inconsequential shack: **Soapy's Parlor,** the headquarters of the notorious gold-rush con man. Unfortunately, the saloon is closed to visitors.

At the **Red Onion Saloon** a call-girl mannequin peers down from the former second-floor brothel, and drinks are served on the original mahogany bar. *Broadway and 2nd Ave., tel. 907/983–2222.*

You can't help but notice the **Arctic Brotherhood Hall**—just up Broadway between 2nd and 3rd avenues—with its curious driftwood-mosaic facade. Inside is the **Skagway Convention and Visitors Bureau** along with public rest rooms.

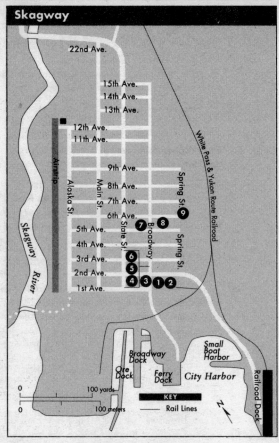

Skagway

22nd Ave.

15th Ave.
14th Ave.
13th Ave.
12th Ave.
11th Ave.
9th Ave.
8th Ave.
7th Ave.
6th Ave.
5th Ave.
4th Ave.
3rd Ave.
2nd Ave.
1st Ave.

Airstrip

Alaska St.

Main St.

State St.

Broadway

Spring St.

Spring St.

Skagway River

White Pass & Yukon Route Railroad

Broadway Dock

Ore Dock

Ferry Dock

City Harbor

Small Boat Harbor

Railroad Dock

0   100 yards
0   100 meters

KEY
Rail Lines

N

Arctic
Brotherhood
Hall 5

Corrington's
Museum of
Alaskan
History 7

Eagles
Hall 8

Golden North
Hotel 6

Klondike Gold
Rush National
Historical Park
Visitor Center . . 1

Red Onion
Saloon 4

Skagway
Museum 9

Soapy's
Parlor 3

White Pass
& Yukon Route
Depot 2

*tel. 907/983–2855 or 888/762–1898, www.skagway.org.
Open daily 8–6.*

6 Built during the 1898 gold rush, the **Golden North Hotel**
was—until closing in 2002—Alaska's oldest hotel. It retains
its gold-rush-era appearance; a golden dome tops the corner cupola. *3rd Ave. and Broadway.*

7 **Corrington's Museum of Alaskan History** is a private collection of exquisitely carved ivory pieces. There's also a gift
shop. *5th Ave. and Broadway, tel. 907/983–2637 or 800/
943–2637. Admission: Free. Open when cruise ships are
in port.*

A rip-roaring revue, "Skagway in the Days of '98," is
staged several times a day at the **Eagles Hall.** Performances
8 are scheduled when cruise ships are in port. *Broadway and
6th Ave., tel. 907/983–2545. Admission: $15.*

9 In the **Skagway Museum** you can see documents relating
to Soapy Smith and Frank Reid, gambling paraphernalia
from the old Board of Trade Saloon, and Native artifacts.
The museum shares a building with the Skagway City Hall,
one block off Broadway. *700 Spring St., tel. 907/983–
2420, www.skagwaymuseum.org. Admission: $2. Open
weekdays 9–5, weekends 1–4.*

Shopping

Broadway is filled with numerous curio shops selling unusual
merchandise. Although prices tend to be high, good deals can
be found, so shop around before making a purchase.

Echoes of Alaska Gallery (Broadway at 4th Ave., tel. 907/
983–2754) has a good selection of regional artwork. One
of the best local galleries is **Hunter Art Studio** (9th Ave. and
Broadway, tel. 888/877–5841), where you will find pieces
by Alaskan artists.

Outdoor Activities and Sports

Real wilderness is within a stone's throw of the docks,
which makes this an excellent hiking port. Try the short
jaunt to beautiful **Lower Dewey Lake.** Start at the corner
of 4th Avenue and Spring Street, go toward the mountain,
cross the footbridge over Pullen Creek, and follow the trail
uphill. It's a 20-minute climb to the lake.

A less strenuous hike is the trip through **Gold Rush Cemetery,** where the epitaphs offer strange but lively bits of social commentary. Infamous villain Soapy Smith has a simple marker; hero Frank Reid has a much larger monument. To get to the cemetery, take the city bus to 23rd Avenue, where a dirt road leads to the graves; it is a 10-minute walk each way. To reach 300-foot-high **Reid Falls,** continue through the cemetery for ¼ mi. The National Park Service Visitor Center offers trail maps; advice; and the helpful brochure *Skagway Gold Rush Cemetery Guide*. Trail maps are also available at the Skagway Convention and Visitors Bureau.

Dining

$$–$$$ ✕ **Olivia's at the Skagway Inn.** An upmarket restaurant in the center of the historic district, Olivia's specializes in freshly caught Alaskan seafood. For lunch there are also delicious homemade seafood, chicken, or beef potpies. A great wine and dessert selection rounds out the menu. *7th Ave. and Broadway, tel. 907/983–3287 or 888/752–4929. MC, V.*

$$–$$$ ✕ **Stowaway Cafe.** Always crowded, this noisy little harborside café is just a few steps from the cruise-ship dock. Not surprisingly, seafood is the attraction—including prawns with Gorgonzola, seafood lasagna, and a hot scallop and bacon salad—but you also can choose tasty steaks, chicken, or smoked ribs. *Congress Way, tel. 907/983–3463. Reservations essential for dinner. AE, MC, V.*

$$ ✕ **Skagway Fish Company.** This small eatery serves fresh seafood, including salmon, oysters, clams, halibut, and prawns for lunch and dinner. Most popular are the halibut fish-and-chips, served with a side of homemade coleslaw. Tables overlooking the harbor surround the central bar. *On waterfront, tel. 907/983–3474. MC, V.*

Saloons

Moe's Frontier Bar (Broadway between 4th and 5th Sts., tel. 907/983–2238) is longtime fixture on the Skagway scene and much frequented by the local folk.

At the **Red Onion Saloon** (Broadway at 2nd St., tel. 907/983–2222) you'll meet as many locals as you will visitors. An impromptu jam with cruise-ship musicians gets under way almost every afternoon. There's live music on Thursday night, ranging from rock and jazz to folk and acoustic.

Tracy Arm

Like Misty Fiords, Tracy Arm and its sister fjord, Endicott Arm, have become staples on many Inside Passage cruises. Ships sail into the arm just before or after a visit to Juneau, 50 mi to the north. A day of scenic cruising in Tracy Arm is a lesson in geology and the forces that shape Alaska. The fjord was carved by a glacier eons ago, leaving behind sheer granite cliffs. Waterfalls continue the process of erosion that the glaciers began. Very small ships may nudge their bows under the waterfalls so crew members can fill pitchers full of glacial runoff. It's a uniquely Alaskan refreshment. Tracy Arm's glaciers haven't disappeared, though; they've just receded, and at the very end of Tracy Arm you'll come to two of them, known collectively as the twin Sawyer Glaciers.

Valdez

Valdez, with its year-round ice-free port, was an entry point for people and goods going to the interior during the gold rush. Today that flow has been reversed, and Valdez Harbor is the southern terminus of the 800-mi (1,290-km) Trans-Alaska pipeline, which carries crude oil from Prudhoe Bay.

Much of Valdez looks relatively modern since the business area was relocated and rebuilt after being destroyed by the 1964 Good Friday earthquake. A few of the old buildings were moved to the new town site.

Many Alaskan communities have summer fishing derbies, but Valdez may hold the record for the number of such contests, stretching from late May into September. The Valdez Silver Salmon Derby begins in late July and runs the entire month of August. Fishing charters abound in this area of Prince William Sound for a good reason: the fertile waters provide some of the best saltwater sportfishing in all of Alaska.

Coming Ashore

Ships tie up at the world's largest floating container dock. About 3 mi from the heart of town, the dock is used not only for cruise ships but also for cargo ships loading with timber and other products bound for markets "outside" (that's what Alaskans call the rest of the world). Ship-organized motor coaches meet you on the pier and provide transportation into town. Cabs and car-rental services will also provide transportation from the pier. Several local ground and adventure-tour operators meet passengers as well.

Once in town, you'll find that Valdez is a very compact community. Almost everything is within easy walking distance of the Valdez Convention and Visitors Bureau in the heart of town. Motor coaches drop passengers at the Visitor Information Center. Taxi service is available, and individualized tours of the area can be arranged with the cab dispatcher.

Exploring Valdez

Sightseeing in Valdez is mostly limited to gazing at the 5,000-foot mountain peaks surrounding the town or to visiting the **Valdez Museum** and its annex. The main building depicts the lives, livelihoods, and events significant to Valdez and surrounding regions. Exhibits include a 1907 steam fire engine, a 19th-century saloon, and a model of the pipeline terminus. *217 Egan Ave., tel. 907/835–2764. Admission: $3. Open daily 8–6.*

The **Valdez Museum Annex** houses exhibits on the 1964 quake, including an impressive replica of the old town and a seismograph showing current activity. *436 S. Hazelet St., tel. 907/835–5407. Admission: $1.50. Open daily 10–6.*

Dining

$–$$$ ✕ **Mike's Palace.** This convivial restaurant is a local favorite. The menu includes veal, terrific pizza, beer-batter halibut, steaks, and Greek gyros. *201 N. Harbor Dr., tel. 907/835–2365. MC, V.*

Vancouver, British Columbia

Cosmopolitan Vancouver has a spectacular setting. Tall fir trees stand practically downtown, the Coast Mountains tower close by, the ocean laps at the doorstep, and people from every corner of the earth create a youthful and vibrant atmosphere.

Vancouver is a young city, even by North American standards. It was not yet a town in 1871, when British Columbia became part of the Canadian confederation. The city's history, such as it is, remains visible to the naked eye: eras are stacked east to west along the waterfront like some century-old archaeological dig—from cobblestone, late-Victorian Gastown to shiny postmodern glass cathedrals of commerce grazing the sunset.

Note that Vancouver is usually the first or last stop on a cruise, unless you're sailing on a longer cruise that begins in Los Angeles or San Francisco.

Coming Ashore

Most ships dock downtown at the Canada Place cruise-ship terminal—instantly recognizable by its rooftop of dramatic white sails and a few minutes' walk from the city center. A few vessels tie up at the Ballantyne cruise terminal, a 10- to 15-minute, $12 cab ride from downtown. Stop off at the **Vancouver Tourist InfoCentre** (200 Burrard St., tel. 604/683–2000) across the street from Canada Place and next door to the Fairmont Waterfront Hotel to pick up brochures on Vancouver attractions and events before leaving the pier area.

Many sights of interest are concentrated in the hemmed-in peninsula of Downtown Vancouver. The heart of Vancouver—which includes the downtown area, Stanley Park, and the West End high-rise residential neighborhood—sits on this peninsula bordered by English Bay and the Pacific Ocean to the west; by False Creek, the inlet home to Granville Island, to the south; and by Burrard Inlet, the working port of the city, to the north, past which loom the North Shore mountains. The oldest part of the city—Gastown and Chinatown—lies at the edge of Burrard Inlet.

There's a taxi stand at the Canada Place cruise-ship terminal; elsewhere, unless you're near a hotel, you'll need to call a taxi service. **Black Top Cabs** (tel. 604/681–2181) is a reliable local cab company. **Yellow Cabs** (tel. 604/681–1111) serves the whole Vancouver area.

Exploring Vancouver

Numbers in the margin correspond to points of interest on the Downtown Vancouver map. Prices are given in Canadian dollars.

① At **Canada Place,** walk around the promenade for fine views of Burrard Inlet, Stanley Park, and the North Shore mountains.

② **Gastown** is where Vancouver originated after "Gassy" Jack Deighton arrived at Burrard Inlet in 1867 with his Native American wife, a barrel of whiskey, and few amenities and set up a saloon to entertain the mill workers living in the area. When the transcontinental train arrived in 1887, Gastown became the transfer point for trade with the Orient and was soon crowded with hotels and warehouses. The Klondike gold rush encouraged further development until 1912, when the "golden years" ended. From the 1930s to the 1950s hotels were converted into rooming houses, and the warehouse district shifted elsewhere. The neglected area gradually became run-down. However, both Gastown and Chinatown were declared historic districts in the late 1970s and have been revitalized. Gastown is now chockablock with boutiques, cafés, and souvenir shops. The world's only steam-powered clock, at the corner of Water and Cambie streets, is a popular photo stop. The **Storyeum** (142 Water St., tel. 888/786–7938, www.storyeum.com; admission May–Oct. C$22, Nov.– Apr. C$20; open May–Oct., daily 9–7, tours every ½ hr; Nov.–Apr., daily 10–6, tours every hr) is set to open in spring 2004. This major new attraction will bring Western Canada's history to life through multimedia presentations, live theater, and life-size sets.

The Chinese were among the first inhabitants of Vancouver, and some of the oldest buildings in the city are in **③** **Chinatown.** A sizable Chinese community had settled in British Columbia after the 1858 Cariboo gold rush, but the greatest influx from China came in the 1880s, when 15,000 laborers arrived to help construct the Canadian Pacific Railway. Highlights of a visit to Chinatown include the **Dr. Sun Yat-Sen Classical Chinese Garden** (578 Carrall St., tel. 604/662–3207; admission C$8.25; open May–mid-June and Sept., daily 10–6; mid-June–Aug., daily 9:30–7; Oct.–

Apr., Tues.–Sun. 10–4:30), the first authentic Ming Dynasty–style garden built outside of China.

The **Chinese Cultural Centre Museum and Archives** (555 Columbia St., tel. 604/658–8880; admission C\$4, free Tues.; open Tues.–Sun. 11–5) is an art gallery and museum dedicated to Chinese-Canadian culture.

The fastest route from Gastown to Chinatown passes through a rough part of town, so it's better to take a taxi between the two areas.

❹ **Stanley Park** is a 1,000-acre wilderness park just blocks from downtown. An afternoon in Stanley Park gives you a capsule tour of Vancouver that includes beaches, the ocean, the harbor, Douglas fir and cedar forests, and a good look at the North Shore mountains. The park sits on a peninsula, and along the shore is a 9-km-long (6-mi-long) bicycle and pedestrian pathway called the Seawall. This seaside pathway extends another 2 km (1 mi) to the Canada Place cruise-ship terminal, so you could start your walk or ride from there. Bicycles are for rent on the waterfront just west of Canada Place and at Georgia and Denman streets near the park entrance. Cyclists must wear helmets and ride in a counterclockwise direction. **Stanley Park Horse-Drawn Tours** (tel. 604/681–5115) offers hour-long narrated tours of the park between mid-March and the end of October. The free **Stanley Park Shuttle** (tel. 604/257–8400) operates from mid-June to mid-September.

Inside the park are several restaurants, a children's miniature railway and petting zoo, several sandy beaches, an outdoor pool, and a network of trails through old-growth forest. At the **Vancouver Aquarium Marine Science Centre** (845 Avison Way, Stanley Park, tel. 604/659–3474, www.vanaqua.org; admission C\$15.95; open July–Labor Day, daily 9:30–7; Labor Day–June, daily 10–5:30), within the park grounds, you can see whale shows, plus sea life from around the world.

Taxis to Stanley Park cost about C\$8 one-way from Canada Place, Gastown, or Chinatown (*see* Coming Ashore, *above,* for taxi companies). You can also catch a west-bound bus at the corner of Pender and Granville streets, a few blocks north of the cruise-ship terminal. The

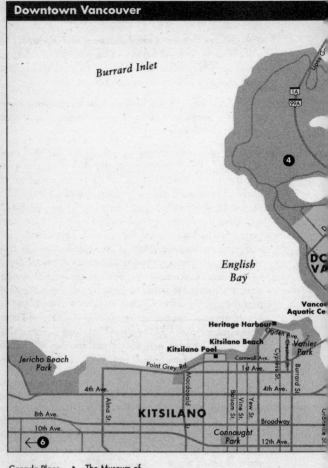

Burrard Inlet

English Bay

Heritage Harbour

Kitsilano Beach

Kitsilano Pool

Jericho Beach Park

Point Grey Rd.

Cornwall Ave.

1st Ave.

4th Ave.

4th Ave.

8th Ave.

10th Ave.

KITSILANO

Connaught Park

Broadway

12th Ave.

Vancou Aquatic Ce

Vanier Park

DO VA

Canada Place . . **1**
Chinatown **3**
Gastown **2**
Granville
Island **5**

The Museum of
Anthropology . . **6**
Stanley Park . . . **4**

bus is marked STANLEY PARK, and the fare is C$2 each way. For information, call 604/953–3333.

A 15-minute cab ride or a short hop on a foot-passenger ferry (tel. 604/689–5858 or 604/684–7781) will take you to

❺ **Granville Island,** south of downtown. A former industrial area refurbished in the 1970s as an urban park, it's now one of Vancouver's liveliest spots, with a huge public market, art galleries and crafts shops, and several museums and theaters. For information contact the **Granville Island Information Centre** (tel. 604/666–5784, www.granvilleisland.com).

❻ **The Museum of Anthropology** is a little out of the way (about 30 minutes by taxi from Canada Place), but it's a must-see for anyone with an interest in the region's aboriginal cultures. Set in a striking building overlooking the Pacific, the museum has one of the world's leading collections of Pacific Northwest First Nations art. *6393 N.W. Marine Dr., on University of British Columbia campus, tel. 604/822–3825, www.moa.ubc.ca. Admission: C$9. Open Memorial Day–Labor Day, Tues. 10–9, Wed.–Mon. 10–5; Labor Day–Memorial Day, Tues. 11–9, Wed.–Sun. 11–5.*

Shopping

Unlike that of many cities where suburban malls have taken over, Vancouver's downtown still has plenty of individual boutiques and specialty shops. Stores are usually open Monday, Tuesday, Wednesday, and Saturday 9:30–6; Thursday and Friday 9:30–9; and Sunday noon–5.

Save your receipts to receive a 7% GST tax refund from the Canadian government when you leave Canada. Ask for a form at customs; many Vancouver shops also have GST refund forms. **Global Refund** (900 W. Georgia St., tel. 604/893–8478), on the lower level of the Fairmont Hotel Vancouver, can give you an on-the-spot cash GST refund, though it charges a 20% commission.

Robson Street, stretching from Burrard to Bute Street, is full of small boutiques and cafés. Vancouver's liveliest street is not only for the fashion-conscious; it also provides many excellent corners for people-watching and attracts an array of street performers.

You'll also find designer shops in and around **Sinclair Centre** (757 W. Hastings St., at Granville St.), just a block south of the Canada Place cruise-ship terminal.

Chinatown—centered on Pender and Main streets—is an exciting and animated area with exotic food stores and import shops. Asian tea and herbal products are stocked at **Ten Lee Hong Tea and Ginseng** (500 Main St., tel. 604/689–7598). At **Ten Ren Tea and Ginseng Company** (550 Main St., tel. 604/684–1566) you can sample exotic tea blends. For art, ceramics, and rosewood furniture, take a look at **Yeu Hua Handicraft Ltd.** (173 E. Pender St., tel. 604/662–3832). If you are staying overnight on a weekend, check out the **Chinatown Night Market**—a street market running from 6:30 PM to 11 PM Friday, Saturday, and Sunday from May to September—along Keefer, East Pender, and East Georgia streets between Main and Gore streets.

Chapters (788 Robson St., tel. 604/682–4066) has an excellent selection of books and magazines, including Canadian and British editions of books that may be hard to find in the States. For used and antiquarian books, try **MacLeod's Books** (455 W. Pender St., tel. 604/681–7654).

Some of the best places in Vancouver for good-quality souvenirs (West Coast Native art, books, music, jewelry, and so on) are the museum and gallery gift shops. The **Clamshell Gift Shop** (tel. 604/659–3413) at the aquarium in Stanley Park has souvenir clothing and aquatic-theme toys and gifts. The **Gallery Store** (in Vancouver Art Gallery, 750 Hornby St., tel. 604/662–4706) has a good selection of art books and locally designed jewelry. **Hill's Native Art** (165 Water St., tel. 604/685–4249) has Vancouver's largest selection of First Nations art. In Gastown, Northwest Coast Native and Inuit art is available at **Images for a Canadian Heritage** (164 Water St., tel. 604/685–7046 or 877/212–8900). The **Inuit Gallery of Vancouver** (206 Cambie St., tel. 604/688–7323 or 888/615–8399) exhibits Northwest Coast and Inuit art. **Salmon Village** (779 Thurlow St., tel. 604/685–3378), off Robson Street's main shopping strip, has all manner of travel-ready Canadian delicacies, from maple syrup to salmon.

Outdoor Activities and Sports

BIKING

Vancouver's 23-mi (37-km) **Seawall bicycle path** starts at Canada Place and continues, with a few detours, around Stanley Park and False Creek to the south shore of English Bay. The Stanley Park section is the most popular. Rentals are available near the park entrance from **Bayshore Bicycles** (745 Denman St., tel. 604/688–2453). **Spokes Bicycle Rentals** (1798 W. Georgia St., tel. 604/688–5141), at Denman and Georgia near Stanley Park, has mountain, kids', and tandem bikes and also runs group bike tours. If you're cycling from Canada Place, you can rent bikes and Rollerblades from **Harbour Air Adventure Centre** (1081 Coal Harbour Rd., tel. 604/233–3500) to the west of Canada Place where the floatplanes dock.

GOLF

The **Furry Creek Golf and Country Club** (Hwy. 99, Furry Creek, tel. 604/922–9576) is a mountain- and ocean-view course about 45 minutes north of Vancouver. For a spur-of-the-moment game, call **Last Minute Golf** (tel. 604/878–1833 or 800/684–6344). The company matches golfers and courses at substantial greens-fees discounts. The **Westwood Plateau Golf and Country Club** (3251 Plateau Blvd., Coquitlam, tel. 604/552–0777) is a mountainside course about 45 minutes east of town.

Dining

$–$$$$ ✕ **Imperial Chinese Seafood.** This elegant Cantonese restaurant in the art deco Marine Building has stupendous views of Stanley Park and the North Shore mountains through two-story floor-to-ceiling windows. Any dish with lobster, crab, or shrimp from the live tanks is recommended, as is the dim sum, served daily 11–2:30. *355 Burrard St., tel. 604/688–8191. DC, MC, V.*

$$–$$$ ✕ **Aqua Riva.** This lofty, lively modern room just yards from the Canada Place cruise-ship terminal has striking views over the harbor and the North Shore mountains. Food from the wood-fired oven, rotisserie, and grill includes thin-crust pizzas with innovative toppings, grilled salmon, and spit-roasted chicken. Lunch brings a good selection of salads, sandwiches, and salmon dishes. A microbrew and martini

list rounds out the menu. *200 Granville St., tel. 604/683–5599. AE, DC, MC, V. No lunch weekends.*

$$–$$$ ✕**Umberto Borgo Antico Al Porto.** Terra-cotta tiles and archways grace this Gastown restaurant's lower floor; upstairs, tall windows overlook the harbor. Borgo Antico serves such Tuscan dishes as grilled calamari salad, gnocchi with artichokes and sun-dried tomatoes, veal medallions with lemon and capers, and osso buco with risotto. *321 Water St., tel. 604/683–8376. AE, DC, MC, V. Closed Sun. No lunch Sat.*

$$–$$$ **Water Street Café.** The tables at this popular Gastown café spill out onto the sidewalk for front-row views of the steam clock across the street. Choose among crab chowder or more than a dozen varieties of pasta, or treat yourself to plate of Fanny Bay oysters. Breads are baked in-house. *300 Water St., tel. 604/689–2832, AE, MC, V,*

$ ✕**Incendio.** Thin-crust pizzas and mix-and-match pastas and sauces draw crowds to this Gastown eatery, set in a circa-1900 building, with exposed brick, local artwork, and big curved windows. *103 Columbia St., tel. 604/688–8694. AE, MC, V. No lunch weekends.*

Pubs

Vancouver's pubs are good places for a drink with a view or a casual meal. Many of them brew their own beer, and the food is at least as good as what you'd find in a similarly priced restaurant. Smoking is banned indoors in all the city's bars and pubs. Pub patrons must be at least 19 years old, but many pubs have separate restaurant sections where all ages are welcome.

Try the **Irish Heather** (217 Carrall St., tel. 604/688–9779) for a pint of properly poured Guinness. An upstairs restaurant serves Irish food, and out back is a **Shebeen,** or whiskey house, where you can sample any of about 130 whiskies. At **Steamworks** (375 Water St., tel. 604/689–2739), on the edge of Gastown, they use an age-old steam brewing process and large copper kettles (visible through glass walls in the restaurant downstairs) to whip up six to nine different brews. There's a restaurant on the lower level. The lively, singles-scene **Yaletown Brewing Company** (1111 Mainland St., tel. 604/681–2739) is based in a huge renovated warehouse with a glassed-in brewery turning out eight microbrews; it also has a darts and billiards pub and a restaurant with an open-grill kitchen.

On Granville Island **Bridges** (1696 Duranleau St., tel. 604/687–4400) has the city's biggest marina-side deck and a cozy, nautical-theme pub.

Victoria, British Columbia

Though Victoria is not in Alaska, it is a port of call for many ships cruising the Inside Passage. Just like the communities of Southeast Alaska, Victoria had its own gold-rush stampede in the 1800s, when 25,000 miners flocked to British Columbia's Cariboo country. Today the city is a mix of stately buildings and English traditions. Flower baskets hang from lampposts, shops sell Harris tweed and Irish linen, and visitors sightsee aboard red double-decker buses or horse-drawn carriages. Afternoon tea is still served daily at the city's elegant Empress Hotel. A trip to the beautiful Butchart Gardens, a short drive outside the city, is worthwhile if you have the time.

Coming Ashore

Only the smallest excursion vessels can dock downtown in the Inner Harbour. Ocean liners must tie up at the Ogden Point Cruise Ship Terminal, a C$4–C$5 cab ride from downtown. Metered taxis meet the ship. The **Tourism Victoria Visitor InfoCentre** (812 Wharf St., tel. 250/953–2033) is across the street from the Empress Hotel, in the Inner Harbour.

Most points of interest are within walking distance of the Empress Hotel. For those that aren't, public and private transportation is readily available from the Inner Harbour. The public bus system is excellent; pick up route maps and schedules at the Visitor InfoCentre. Taxi rates are C$2.40 for pickup, C$1.30 per kilometer (½ mi). **Bluebird Taxi** (tel. 250/382–2222) serves the Victoria area. **Victoria Taxi** (tel. 250/383–7111) is another reliable local company.

Exploring Victoria

Numbers in the margin correspond to points of interest on the Inner Harbour, Victoria, map. Prices are given in Canadian dollars.

① Victoria's heart is the **Inner Harbour,** always bustling with ferries, seaplanes, and yachts. In summer the waterfront comes alive with strollers and street entertainers.

② The ivy-covered 1908 **Fairmont Empress Hotel** is the centerpiece of Victoria. A traditional afternoon tea—a full meal of sandwiches, pastries, and scones—is served in the hotel's lavish tea lobby daily. It's something of a tradition here, though it is pricey. *721 Government St., tel. 250/384–8111, 250/389–2727 tea reservations.*

③ The **Crystal Garden Conservation Centre,** built in 1925 under a glass roof as a public saltwater swimming pool, is now a tropical conservatory and aviary, with flamingos, tortoises, macaws, and butterflies. *713 Douglas St., behind Empress Hotel, tel. 250/953–8815. Admission: C$9. Open mid-June–mid-Sept., daily 9–8; mid-Sept.–Oct. and mid-Mar.–mid-June, daily 9–6; Nov.–mid-Mar., daily 9–5.*

④ **Thunderbird Park** displays a ceremonial longhouse (a communal dwelling) and a fine collection of totem poles. *Belleville St., beside Royal British Columbia Museum.*

⑤ Next to Thunderbird Park is the 1852 **Helmcken House,** the city's oldest residence, which has its original Victorian furniture and a display of antique medical instruments. *10 Elliot St., tel. 250/361–0021. Admission: C$5. Open May–Oct., daily 10–5; Nov.–Apr., Thurs.–Mon. noon–4.*

⑥ The superb **Royal British Columbia Museum** will take at least a couple of hours of your time: its exhibits encompass 12,000 years of natural and human history. An on-site IMAX theater shows National Geographic films on a six-story-high screen. *675 Belleville St., tel. 250/356–7226 or 888/447–7977. Admission: $10, IMAX theater $9.75, combination ticket $17.75. Open Museum daily 9–5, theater daily 9–8 (call for show times).*

⑦ The stately, neo-Gothic **British Columbia Parliament Buildings** are constructed of local stone and wood and were opened in 1898. Atop the central dome is a gilded statue of Captain George Vancouver, for whom Vancouver Island was named. Free half-hour tours are offered several times a day year-round. *501 Belleville St., tel. 250/387–3046.*

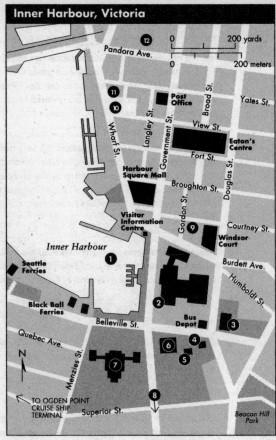

Inner Harbour, Victoria

Pandora Ave.

0 · · · · 200 yards
0 · · · · 200 meters

Post Office
Yates St.
Broad St.
View St.
Eaton's Centre
Fort St.
Wharf St.
Langley St.
Government St.
Douglas St.
Harbour Square Mall
Broughton St.
Gordon St.
Visitor Information Centre
Courtney St.
Windsor Court
Inner Harbour
Burdett Ave.
Humboldt St.
Seattle Ferries
Black Ball Ferries
Belleville St.
Bus Depot
Quebec Ave.
Menzies St.
N

TO OGDEN POINT CRUISE SHIP TERMINAL
Superior St.
Beacon Hill Park

Bastion Square **10**

British Columbia Parliament Buildings . . . **7**

Crystal Garden Conservation Center **3**

Emily Carr House **8**

Fairmont Empress Hotel **2**

Helmcken House **5**

Inner Harbour **1**

Maritime Museum of British Columbia . . **11**

Market Square **12**

Royal British Columbia Museum **6**

Thunderbird Park **4**

Victoria Bug Zoo **9**

Admission: Free. Open mid-May–Labor Day, daily 8:30–5; Labor Day–mid-May, weekdays 8:30–5.

(8) The Victorian **Emily Carr House** was the childhood home of one of Canada's most famous and most beloved artists; Carr's autobiography was used to guide the restoration of the house. *207 Government St., tel. 250/383–5843. Admission: C$5.35. Open mid-May–mid-Oct., daily 10–5; by arrangement rest of yr.*

With its gardens, petting zoo, and great views of the Olympic Mountains, **Beacon Hill Park** is the city's favorite green space. It's east of Douglas Street and south of Southgate Street, just a few blocks from the Inner Harbour. The park is also home to Mile Zero of the Trans-Canada Highway and the world's largest free-standing totem pole.

(9) Just north of the Fairmont Empress hotel is the **Victoria Bug Zoo**, a creepy-crawly attraction popular with kids. Many of the insects—mostly large tropical varieties, such as stick insects, scorpions, and centipedes—can be held; staff members are on hand to dispense scientific information. *631 Courtney St., tel. 250/384–2847, www.bugzoo.bc.ca. Admission: C$6. Open July–Aug., daily 9–9; Sept.–June, Mon.–Sat. 9:30–5:30, Sun. 11–5:30.*

(10) A short walk from the Inner Harbour is **Bastion Square.** Follow Government Street to View Street and you'll see the entrance on your left. Laid out in 1843 as the original site of Ft. Victoria, the atmospheric square is now home to offices and restaurants.

On the north side of Bastion Square, the old courthouse is **(11)** now the **Maritime Museum of British Columbia,** with three floors of nautical-theme exhibits, including a full-scale vice-admiralty courtroom and one of North America's oldest cage lifts. *28 Bastion Sq., tel. 250/385–4222. Admission: C$6. Open daily 9:30–4:30.*

(12) Two blocks north of Bastion Square is **Market Square,** a former staging post for prospectors on their way to the Klondike. It's now an atmospheric courtyard surrounded by boutiques and cafés. From Market Square you can cut up Fan Tan Alley, Canada's narrowest street, to Victoria's historic Chinatown.

Take a taxi (or a shore excursion) to **Butchart Gardens.** In a city of gardens, these 55 acres rank among the most beautiful in the world. In July and August a fireworks display is held every Saturday evening. *22 km (14 mi) north of Victoria off Hwy. 17, tel. 250/652–5256 or 866/652–4422, www.butchartgardens.com. Admission: C$20 mid-June–Sept; rates vary Oct.–mid-June. Open mid-June–Aug., daily 9 AM–10:30 PM; Sept.–mid-June, open daily at 9, closing times vary.*

Shopping

Save your receipts to receive a 7% GST tax refund from the Canadian government when you leave Canada; ask for a form at customs (many shops have the forms as well). Victoria stores specializing in English imports are plentiful, though Canadian-made goods are usually a better buy.

Victoria's main shopping area is along Government Street north of the Empress Hotel. The **Cowichan Trading Co., Ltd.** (1328 Government St., tel. 250/383–0321) sells Northwest Coast Native jewelry, art, and hand-knit Cowichan sweaters. **Hill's Native Art** (1008 Government St., tel. 250/385–3911) sells original West Coast Native artwork. For imported linens and lace, have a look at the **Irish Linen Stores** (1019 Government St., tel. 250/383–6812). **Munro's Books** (1108 Government St., tel. 250/382–2464), in a beautifully restored 1909 building, is one of Canada's prettiest bookstores.

From Government Street turn right onto Fort Street and walk five blocks to **Antique Row,** between Blanshard and Cook streets, where dozens of antiques shops sell books, jewelry, china, furniture, artwork, and collectibles.

Dining

$$$–$$$$ ✕ **The Blue Crab Bar and Grill.** Fresh seafood and expansive harbor views are the draws at this modern, airy restaurant in the Coast Harbourside Hotel. Signature dishes include Dungeness crab and shrimp cakes as well as a scallop and jumbo-prawn sauté, though the daily specials are always tempting. *146 Kingston St., tel. 250/480–1999. AE, D, DC, MC, V.*

$$–$$$$ ✕ **Il Terrazzo.** The locals' choice for alfresco dining, Il Terrazzo has a charming redbrick terrace tucked away off Waddington Alley just north of the Inner Harbour. Dijon-

encrusted rack of lamb, osso buco with porcini mushrooms, and pizzas from the restaurant's wood-burning oven are among the hearty Italian dishes served. *555 Johnson St., tel. 250/361–0028. AE, DC, MC, V. No lunch Sun., or Sat. Oct.–Apr.*

$$ ✕ **Re-Bar Modern Food.** This bright and cheery café in Bastion Square is *the* place for vegetarians in Victoria, though the almond burgers, veggie enchiladas, decadent home-baked goodies, and big breakfasts will keep omnivores happy as well. *50 Bastion Sq., tel. 250/361–9223. AE, MC, V. No dinner Sun.*

$ ✕ **Barb's Place.** This blue take-out shack floats on the quay at Fisherman's Wharf, west of the Inner Harbour and about 1 km (½ mi) from the cruise-ship dock. Cod, halibut, oysters, seafood burgers, chowder, and carrot cake are all prepared fresh on the premises. Ferries sail to Fisherman's Wharf from the Inner Harbour. *Fisherman's Wharf, Erie St., tel. 250/384–6515. Reservations not accepted. MC, V. Closed Nov.–Feb.*

Wrangell

Between Ketchikan and Petersburg lies Wrangell, on an island near the mouth of the mighty Stikine River. The town is off the typical cruise-ship track and is visited mostly by lines with an environmental or educational emphasis, such as Alaska Sightseeing/Cruise West and World Explorer Cruises. This small, unassuming timber and fishing community has lived under three flags since the arrival of the Russian traders. It was known as Redoubt St. Dionysius when it was part of Russian America; then it was called Fort Stikine after the British took it over. It was renamed Wrangell when the Americans purchased it in 1867.

Coming Ashore

Cruise ships calling in to Wrangell dock downtown, within walking distance of the museum and gift stores. Greeters welcome you and are available to answer questions. The small **Wrangell Visitor Center** (tel. 907/874–3901 or 800/367–9745, www.wrangellchamber.org) is next to the dock inside the Stikine Inn.

Wrangell's few attractions—the most notable being totem-filled Chief Shakes Island—are within walking distance of the pier. Petroglyph Beach, where you find rocks marked with mysterious prehistoric symbols, is 1 mi from the pier. Most cruise-ship visitors see it either on a guided shore excursion or by taxi. Call **Porky's Cab Co.** (tel. 907/874–3603) or **Star Cab** (tel. 907/874–3622).

Exploring Wrangell

Numbers in the margin correspond to points of interest on the Wrangell map.

① Walking up Front Street will bring you to **Kiksadi Totem Park,** a pocket park of Alaska greenery and impressive totem poles.

② On your way to Wrangell's number one attraction—Chief Shakes Island—stop at **Chief Shakes's grave site,** uphill from the Wrangell shipyard on Case Avenue. Buried here is Shakes VI, the last of a line of chiefs who bore that name. He led the local Tlingits during the first half of the 19th century. Two killer-whale totems mark the chief's burial place.

③ On **Chief Shakes Island,** reached by a footbridge off the harbor dock, you can see some of the finest totem poles in Alaska, as well as a tribal house constructed in the 1930s as a replica of one that was home to many of the various Shakes and their peoples. There are six totems on the island, two of them more than 100 years old. The original corner posts of the tribal house are in the museum. *tel. 907/874–3747. Admission: $2. Open when cruise ships are in port.*

After your visit to Chief Shakes Island, wander out to the end of the dock for the view and for picture taking at the busy **boat harbor** and the adjacent **seaplane float.**

④ The **Wrangell Museum**'s historical collection includes decorative posts from Chief Shakes's clan house (carved in the late 1700s), Native baskets and masks, items from Russian and English settlers, gold-rush memorabilia, and a fine photo collection. *296 Outer Dr., tel. 907/874–3770. Admission: $4. Open Tues.–Sat. 10–5 and when cruise ships are in port.*

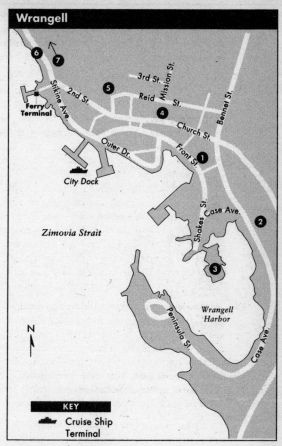

Wrangell

KEY
Cruise Ship
Terminal

Chief
Shakes's
grave site . . . 2
Chief
Shakes
Island 3
Kiksadi
Totem
Park 1
Petroglyph
Beach 6
Wrangell
Public
Library 5
Wrangell
Museum 4

⑤ Outside the **Wrangell Public Library** are a couple of ancient petroglyphs. They are worth seeing if you don't plan to make the trip to Petroglyph Beach. *124 2nd Ave., tel. 907/ 874–3535.*

⑥ **Petroglyph Beach** is undoubtedly one of the more curious sights in Southeast Alaska. Scattered among other rocks along the shore are three dozen or more large stones bearing designs and pictures chiseled by unknown ancient artists. Do not attempt to move any of the petroglyph stones. A boardwalk provides access to the beach and includes signs describing the site, along with carved replicas of the petroglyphs. You are welcome to use these (but not the originals) for rubbings. Most tours provide rice paper and charcoal or crayons for this purpose. *Off Evergreen Ave., 1 mi north of downtown.*

Shopping

A unique souvenir from Wrangell is a natural **garnet,** gathered at Garnet Ledge, facing the Stikine River. These semiprecious gems are sold by the children of Wrangell for 50¢ to $20, depending on their size and quality. You will find their card tables lining the cruise-ship dock.

Dining

Wrangell's dining options are basic and inexpensive, with no standouts.

$$ ✕ **Waterfront Grill.** Your best bet for food in Wrangell is this restaurant inside Stikine Inn where they serve burgers, cross-cut waffle fries, pasta, and homemade pizzas. *107 Front St., tel. 907/874–3388. MC, V.*

4 Shore Excursions

BEFORE YOUR CRUISE, you'll receive a booklet describing the shore excursions your cruise line offers. A few lines let you book excursions in advance; all sell them on board during the cruise. Canceling your excursion may incur penalties, and the amount varies with the number of days remaining until the tour. These trips have limited capacity and are sold on a first-come, first-served basis.

Among the many options available, there are some "musts." Experience an outdoor adventure at least once during your cruise—you don't have to be athletically inclined to raft down a river or paddle a sea kayak along the coastline. Go to an evening salmon feast, where you'll savor freshly caught fish cooked over an open fire. And consider a helicopter or small-plane tour. Flightseeing is expensive, and it can be dangerous, but it's the best way to grasp the expansiveness and grandeur of the land, and it's the only way to reach remote parts of Alaska. Before you fly, contact your cruise line's representative, or the air tour operator itself, to check how long the company has been in service, its accident/incident statistics, and its safety procedures. If possible, try to meet with and talk to your pilot before the trip. Know where you're going and how long the trip will take. Avoid trips with long stopovers in remote areas—drastic weather changes can result in the cancellation or complication of your return flight. Pay attention to the safety message at the start of the flight, noting especially the location of emergency survival gear. Long distances, mountainous terrain, and challenging weather conditions are all hazardous factors, but pilot error, sometimes due to passenger interference, is often involved. Never push a pilot to do what he or she is reluctant to do, such as circle low over a bear, and never pressure him to hurry up and get back to the ship. Missing the departure of your ship is much better than pushing a pilot to fly when weather conditions are unsafe.

Cruise-line shore-excursion booklets present a variety of options, and many companies provide detailed descriptions of tours on their Web sites. We have compiled a selection below of the most worthwhile excursions to help you make your choices. Not all those listed below are offered by all cruise lines. Prices will vary.

You can also arrange many of these tours through the visitor-information counter in each port. These counters are usually close to the pier. *See* Coming Ashore *in each port of call section in* Chapter 3 for exact locations.

Haines

The small coastal community of Haines was originally settled by the Tlingit Indians and is known for the work of its local artists, native dancers, and, in fall and winter, large numbers of bald eagles. If your cruise ship only stops in nearby Skagway, you can catch a fast catamaran (around $80 round-trip) for a day away from the crowds.

Adventure/Scenic

Chilkat Bald Eagle Preserve Float Trip. A raft trip through the Chilkat Bald Eagle Preserve introduces you to some eagles and—if you're lucky—a moose or a bear. The trip starts with a 30-minute guided van tour through Chilkat Valley to the heart of the preserve. Then you board rafts for a gentle, scenic float trip down the Chilkat River (no children under age seven). In October, the trees are filled with some 3,000 bald eagles. *3½ hrs. $100.*

Chilkat Bicycle Adventure. Tour Haines by mountain bike with a knowledgeable guide. This tour includes a visit to the century-old buildings of Fort Seward and a ride along the lower Chilkat River, home to nesting bald eagles. *1½ hrs. $50.*

Chilkat Rain Forest Nature Hike. Explore a lush Alaskan rain forest on this 3-mi guided hike along Chilkoot Inlet. The path is easy and well-maintained, and spotting scopes are provided to watch for bald eagles, mountain goats, and other wildlife along the way. *3 hrs. $85.*

Tastes of Alaska

Haines Salmon Bake. Savor locally caught salmon served potlatch-style in a native longhouse. *1 hr. $35.*

Juneau

Alaska's capital, Juneau is a picturesque mix of the old and new. Buildings from the early 1900s line the main road

(Franklin Street), while new Victorian-style structures spread south along the cruise ship docks. The city's historic center is easy to see on foot, though the hills make walking more challenging if you wander. Try to get to the Mendenhall Glacier, one of Alaska's "drive-up" glaciers, which is 13 mi (21 km) outside town.

Adventure

Exploring Glaciers by Helicopter and Dog Sled. Fly deep into the Juneau Icefield by helicopter on this high-adventure excursion. A guide greets you when you land and explains dogsledding, then takes you on a sled ride across the snow-covered glacier. Return to Juneau by helicopter, with additional flightseeing en route. *3 hrs. $360–$420.*

Mendenhall River Rafting. Professional rafters row you down the Mendenhall River through alternating stretches of calm water and gentle rapids. Rubber rain boots, protective clothing, and life jackets are provided. Children love this one (the minimum age is six years). *3½ hrs. $110.*

Pilot's Choice Helicopter Flightseeing. One of the most popular helicopter glacier tours in Alaska includes a landing on the Juneau Icefield for a walk on a glacier. Boots and rain gear are provided. *3 hrs. $300.*

Tram and Guided Alpine Walk. You start with a short tour of downtown Juneau, then ride up the Mt. Roberts Tramway on this very popular trip. Once you reach the top—1,800 ft over the city—a guide takes you through pristine rain forest and alpine meadows. The hike is ¾ mi (1¼ km) over gravel and boardwalk trails and is conducted in all weather conditions. Sturdy, comfortable walking shoes and warm, waterproof clothing are advised. You can return via the tram at any time. *2½ hrs. $50.*

Scenic

Gold Panning and Gold Mine Tour. Pan for gold with a prospector guide and tour the entrance area of the Alaska-Juneau mine. This is great for children. *1½ hrs. $42–$45.*

Grand Tour of Juneau. Take this bus excursion to see Mendenhall Glacier, spawning salmon at the Macauley Salmon Hatchery, and the Glacier Gardens rain forest. *4¼ hrs. $80–$90.*

Tastes of Alaska

Floatplane Ride and Taku Glacier Lodge Salmon Bake. Fly over the Juneau Icefield to rustic Taku Glacier Lodge, where you can dine on outstanding barbecued salmon. Afterward, explore the virgin rain forest or relax in the lodge. The tour is expensive, but it consistently gets rave reviews. *3 hrs. $235–$240.*

Gold Creek Salmon Bake. Alaska king salmon barbecued over an open fire is included at this all-you-can-eat outdoor meal. After dinner, you can walk in the woods, explore an abandoned mine, or pan for gold. *1½–2 hrs. $31–$35.*

Ketchikan

This is one of the best places to sign on for a fishing charter. Ketchikan is also known for its authentic totem poles and nearby Misty Fiords National Monument, one of Alaska's grandest sights to see by plane.

Adventure

Misty Fiords by Floatplane. Aerial views of granite cliffs that rise 4,000 ft from the sea, waterfalls, rain forests, and wildlife are topped off with a landing on a high wilderness lake. *2 hrs. $217–$220.*

Misty Fiords Wilderness Cruise and Flight. See this beautiful area from the air and sea on a 20-minute floatplane trip and a 2¾-hour cruise. The plane lands in the heart of the wilderness where you climb on a small boat for the narrated voyage back to Ketchikan. *4 hrs. $260–$270.*

Sportfishing. Cast your line for Alaska king and silver salmon or halibut along the Inside Passage. All equipment is provided, and you can buy your license on board. Group size is limited. Fish will be cleaned, and arrangements can be made to have your catch frozen or smoked and shipped home. *5 hrs. $180–$185.*

Tatoosh Islands Sea Kayaking. A scenic drive to Knudson Cove is followed by a boat ride to Tatoosh Islands, where you board an easy-to-paddle sea kayak for a whale's-eye view of a remote part of Tongass National Forest. The minimum age is seven. *4 hrs. $130.*

Cultural

Great Alaskan Lumberjack Show. See Southeast Alaska's logging history in action with events like springboard chopping, buck sawing, axe throwing, log rolling, and tree climbing. The production is hackneyed but always popular. *1½ hrs. $29.*

Saxman Native Village. Learn about the Tlingit culture in this native village with more than 20 totem poles. You can watch totem-pole carvers and a theatrical production in the Beaver Clan House. *2½ hrs. $48–$50.*

Totem Bight and Ketchikan City Tour. Visit the bustling center of Ketchikan and Totem Bight State Park to the north, where totem poles and a native clan house face the saltwater. *2½ hrs. $36–$39.*

Petersburg

The fishing community of Petersburg, with its Scandinavian-style homes, still reflects the heritage of the Norwegians who settled here in the late 19th century.

Scenic

LeConte Glacier Flightseeing. One of the best flightseeing tours in Alaska takes you to the southernmost calving glacier in North America. *45-min flight. $170.*

Little Norway. Here's a chance to explore this pretty fishing town by bus and watch a Scandinavian dance performance at the Sons of Norway Hall. Some tours also include a Norwegian-style smorgasbord. *2 hrs. $30.*

Waterfront Walking Tour. A guide will relate the history and fishing heritage of Petersburg as you explore the old part of town on foot. *1½ hrs. $10.*

Seward

This tiny town, nestled against the mountains on Prince William Sound, is the primary port for cruise travelers heading to or from Anchorage. The town is one of Alaska's oldest and most scenic, but the real attractions are in the surrounding wilderness.

Adventure

Godwin Glacier Dog Sled Tour. These tours begin with a 15-minute helicopter ride to remote Godwin Glacier. Here you step onto the ice and learn about mushing from an Iditarod veteran, meet the dogs, and head out across the glacier by dog sled. *1½ hrs. $380–$400.*

Scenic

Portage Glacier. Passengers disembarking in Seward often take advantage of the chance to see Portage Glacier while en route to Anchorage. The drive along Turnagain Arm to Portage Glacier is one of Alaska's most beautiful. A boat transports you to the glacial face, which has receded dramatically in recent years. *1-hr boat tour. $35–$40.*

Resurrection Bay Cruise. Boats depart from the Seward harbor and cruise near Bear Glacier and past playful sea otters, a sea lion rookery, and nesting seabirds (including puffins). Whales are commonly sighted, too. *3½ hrs. $72.*

Sitka

Sitka was the capital of Russian Alaska. Good walkers can easily see the town on foot, but consider taking the town tour so you don't miss the eagle hospital and the 15 totem poles and towering trees of Sitka National Historical Park.

Adventure

Sea Life Discovery Semi-Submersible. Large underwater windows on this vessel let you see Sitka Sound's kelp forests, fish, and crab. You can get an even closer look from the underwater camera images displayed on the boat's video monitor. *2 hrs. $80.*

Sitka by Sea Kayak. Kayak Sitka's coastline against the backdrop of the Mt. Edgecumb volcano. *3 hrs. $100.*

Sportfishing. Try for the abundant salmon and halibut in these waters. All equipment is provided; you buy your license on board. Your catch can be frozen and shipped. *3½ hrs. $180.*

Cultural

History and Nature Walking Tour. A guided walk through Sitka details its political and natural history. This tour includes all the major sites plus a visit to the Sitka National Historic Park for a stroll through the rain forest, and time at the Raptor Rehabilitation Center. Return downtown by van. *2½ hrs. $45–$50.*

Native Cultural Tour. A Native Alaskan guides you on this informative bus tour. Stops include Sitka National Historic Park and Sheldon Jackson Museum as well as a performance by the Naa Kahidi Dancers in a traditional-style clan house. *2½ hrs. $42.*

Russian-America Tour. Stops at Castle Hill, the Russian Cemetery, St. Michael's Cathedral, and Sitka National Historic Park are included in this bus tour of Sitka's rich Russian heritage. The finale is a Russian-style folk-dance performance by the New Archangel Dancers, local women who have mastered the timing and athletic feats required for this traditional style of dance. *2½ hrs. $35–$38.*

Scenic

Sea Otter Quest. This search for the sea otter and other Sitka wildlife is a cruise-passenger favorite. Creatures that you're likely to see from the boat include whales, eagles, puffins, and more. *3 hrs. $110.*

Skagway

The wooden sidewalks and false-front buildings of Skagway, once the gateway to the Klondike, evoke images of gold-rush fever. The White Pass & Yukon Railroad excursion gives you the chance to get high into the mountains.

Adventure

Heli-Hike Glacier Trek. The helicopter flight that begins this popular trip is followed by a 4-mi hike to Laughton Glacier. Return to Skagway on the famous White Pass & Yukon Route Railway. Participants must be in strong physical condition. *5½ hrs. $300–$315.*

Hike and Float the Chilkoot Trail. This trips opens with a guided van tour to the historic gold-rush townsite of Dyea, start of the historic Chilkoot Trail. From here you hike 2 mi along the Taiya River, then board rafts for an easy 40-minute float back to Dyea. No children under seven are allowed. *4¼ hrs. $100.*

Klondike Bicycle Tour. Ride a van to the top of the Klondike Pass and then bike 15 mi downhill, taking in the spectacular views of White Pass and Alaska's scenery along the way. Stops are made to take photographs of the area's glaciers, coastal mountains, and waterfalls. *2½ hrs. $78–82.*

Cultural/Scenic

Haines Highlights and Lynn Fjord Cruise. Escape the crowds in Skagway on a fast ferry that crosses Lynn Fjord to the scenic town of Haines. Tour historic Fort Seward and the Sheldon Museum; visit a restored fish canning line from the 1950s; and ride up the Chilkat River Valley. Return by ferry to Skagway in time to catch your ship. *6 hrs. $100.*

Skagway Streetcar. Ride in the Skagway Streetcar Company's vintage 1930s cars through town to the Gold Rush Cemetery and Reid Falls, accompanied by a knowledgeable tour guide dressed in Victorian-style costume. *2 hrs. $37–40.*

White Pass & Yukon Railroad. The 20-mi trip in vintage railroad cars—on narrow-gauge tracks built to serve the Yukon goldfields—skims along the edge of granite cliffs; crosses a 215-ft-high, steel-cantilever bridge over Dead Horse Gulch; climbs to 2,865 ft at White Pass Summit; and zigzags through dramatic scenery—including the actual Trail of '98, worn into the mountainside a century ago. *3½ hrs. $95.*

Vancouver, British Columbia

Unless you're on a longer cruise that begins in Los Angeles or San Francisco, Vancouver may likely be your first or last stop. If you're sailing round-trip, you'll get on and off the ship in Vancouver. Because most passengers are busy transferring between the airport and the ship, few shore excursions are scheduled, although some lines offer sightseeing tours as part of the airport transfer. If you plan to stay in Vancouver before or after your cruise, most lines sell pre- or post-cruise city packages.

For cruise passengers on longer cruises, a call in Vancouver will be much like any other port call: you'll disembark just for the day and have the option of taking a ship-organized tour or exploring independently.

Cultural

City Tour. If this is your first visit to Vancouver, consider a city tour, a convenient way to see all the sights of this cosmopolitan city—the largest you'll visit on an Alaska cruise. Highlights include the Gastown district, Chinatown, and Stanley Park. If your cruise terminates in Vancouver, this may be offered as a combined tour and airport transfer, finishing at Vancouver International Airport. *2½–3 hrs. US$31 or US$16 with prepaid airport transfer.*

Some cruise lines offer a longer tour that includes a ride to the top of Grouse Mountain on an aerial tramway and a visit to the gardens of Queen Elizabeth Park. The airport transfer is not usually a part of this package. *4–5 hrs. US$49.*

Vancouver Pre- or Post-Cruise Package. Cruise-line land packages are an easy way to extend your cruise vacation without making separate arrangements. Usually, you'll have a choice of one, two, or three nights in town. Often, you'll also have a choice of hotels in different price ranges. Most packages include sightseeing tours and transfers between the ship and the hotel. Meals are generally extra unless noted in the brochure; transfers between the airport and hotel may be included only for air-sea passengers.

Victoria, British Columbia

Victoria is best known for its British traditions and gardens, which are the focal point of the most popular shore excursions.

Cultural/Scenic

Grand City Drive and Afternoon High Tea. A good choice for Anglophiles, this drive explores Victoria's British heritage. Sights along the route include downtown, Craigdarroch Castle, and residential areas. British-style high tea at a hotel caps off the tour. A variation of this excursion substitutes a tour of the castle for high tea. *4 hrs. US$58.*

Short City Tour and Butchart Gardens. Drive through key places of interest, such as the city center and residential areas, on the way to the spectacular Butchart Gardens, which grows more than 700 varieties of flowers. Stay until evening to witness the romantic nighttime illumination of the gardens. *3½–4 hrs. US$52.*

INDEX